Contents

Preface

This is a complementary handbook to my previous work *Adult Faith: Growing in Wisdom and Understanding* (2010) but can be read and used apart from it. Although the notion of adult-based faith sounds exciting and empowering for many people, it proves quite a quandary for those seeking to ground their newly evolving sense of meaning and holiness. And often they are reluctant to turn to the former resources of church or parish for support and guidance. The anticipation of not being heard or being misunderstood is very real for many adult faith seekers of our time.

This book is not a how-to manual, but rather a resource that will enable adults to discern more deeply what they are experiencing and develop a vocabulary to articulate their inner processes, thus making it easier for the seeker to tell his or her emerging story in mutual conversation or in support group exploration. The book provides several lists that can be used to access and understand one or another aspect of the awakening experience.

I am not offering hand-me-down answers, which is precisely what many adults are seeking to outgrow. However, this leaves the adult seeker with renewed responsibility to come up not merely with a sense of individual resolution to life's big questions, but with a discerning wisdom that can be checked, challenged, and validated in the dialogical forums of spiritual accompaniment or empowering group process. This is quite new territory for adult faith development, and I hope that the ideas outlined in this book will support and encourage adults in their ongoing exploration.

Chapter One

The Meaning of Adult Faith

I become who I will be within the network of relations, rooted in the non-human, blooming in the intimate, branching into the unknown.

— Catherine Keller

In November 1959, a diverse group of scholars gathered at the University of Chicago to celebrate the centennial publication of Charles Darwin's *On the Origin of Species.* Among the keynote speakers was Julian Huxley, son of the famous English biologist, Thomas Henry Huxley. Addressing the audience, Julian Huxley declared that religion as we know it had become a nonadaptive resource, dying because of overreliance on an outdated supernaturalism. "Evolutionary man," he declared, "can no longer take refuge from his loneliness in the arms of a divinized father . . . nor escape from the responsibility of making decisions by sheltering

1

under the umbrella of divine authority." He concluded his address with these words: "Finally, the evolutionary vision is enabling us to discern, however incompletely, the lineaments of a new religion that will arise to serve the needs of the coming age."

Standing on the cusp of the 1960s, Huxley read the evolving religious conscious with remarkable wisdom and insight. The next decade evidenced a kind of religious revival unseen for several decades. We witnessed rebellion and revival, Jesus freaks and oriental mysticism. At a more subtle level, a new consciousness was evolving—whether driven by Darwinian insight or some other more elusive force—and it would exert on religious practice an irreversible trend toward greater questioning, exploring, and adult engagement with life's great questions.

Passing on the Faith

As late as the 1960s, catechists, preachers, and teachers targeted late adolescence as the threshold of religious maturity. If the seeds of faith were not well sown—and already sprouting—by one's eighteenth birthday, religious faith was unlikely to flourish thereafter. Once that goal had been attained, it was assumed that faith had been internalized to a degree that would sustain people throughout their adult years, right up to the moment of death. The critical issue was *psychology* rather than *religion*. By one's eighteenth birthday, human character was molded into what would be its fundamental essence for the rest of the life cycle. What a person had become by late adolescence was widely understood to remain the bedrock of all later growth and development. This idea is now understood to be a rather archaic view of developmental growth, but it still holds sway in the proselytizing strategy of several world religions.

In this framework faith was understood to be set of doctrines—truths to be intellectually assimilated—that made sense for those blessed by the gift of religious belief. If one had been baptized and had received the sacraments of Penance, Eucharist, and Confirmation, it was assumed that one had been blessed with the grace of being a religious believer. Therefore, by one's eighteenth birthday, everything was in place to sustain and nurture faith for the rest of one's life. That same faith acquired in childhood and throughout the adolescent years would remain unchanged for one's entire adult existence.

Passing on the faith came to be understood as a form of indoctrination, in which seniors passed on to juniors a set of truths deemed to be unassailable. Central to such truths was the all-powerful, governing God who issued commandments to be obeyed and a set of beliefs that were never to be questioned. Divine truth from on high was invested in divinely chosen males who ensured that the patriarchal line of command was followed in submissive obedience. God, working through the chosen males, occupied the top of the pyramid; those who submitted, the believers, constituted the bulk of the people at the base. Passivity, based on doctrinal acquiescence and submissive obedience, characterized true holiness. The demarcation line between those possessing truth and those to whom it had to be imparted was crystal clear, and that line should never be transgressed.

To the contemporary reader, it sounds strange, archaic to the point of defying all sense of adult maturity. The reader needs to remember that this same patriarchal mind-set featured in several aspects of the imperial consciousness of the nineteenth and twentieth centuries. Its most extreme expression was that of the slavery system. Because this codependent culture was so pervasive, very few questioned its meaningfulness and when they did they were promptly and efficiently ostracized.

Forth Comes the Adult

As Julian Huxley intimated at the Chicago conference, the 1960s marked a new evolutionary awakening. People all over the world began to rebel and sought to overthrow the old colonialism, the passivity, and the subservience. We were witnessing not merely a human rebellion, but rather a cultural uprising instigated by evolution itself. So new was the concept of *evolution* that few in the religious domain began using the word for at least another decade. By that stage, the evolutionary awakening had become a cultural revolution. Petrified religions and churches reverted to panic mode hoping to salvage the enduring truth of earlier times. It was too late. As Julian Huxley intimated, evolution was giving birth to something akin to a new religion.

The accelerated evolutionary growth of the 1970s and 1980s would produce not a new religion but something a great deal more complex. Remember Teilhard de Chardin: *evolution advances into greater complexity*. World religions morphed into a range of new expressions, not just among the youth; the new developments were significantly pioneered by people of adult years. Think of the inspiring gray-bearded Bede Griffiths in his Christian-Hindu ashram, or Dorothy Day as a mature woman in the United States, who grounded Christian justice in daily life. Of greater impact, however, was the emerging convergence that came to be known as *spirituality*, synthesizing various religious insights such as meditation practices and new age rituals, and transcending the sacred versus secular dualism to forge empowering coalitions with science, cosmology, and indigenous cultures.

Central to many such endeavors was a new type of adult. Some were merely in their twenties, others in their eighties, and careful research would probably indicate that the majority were mid-lifers ("baby-boomers" as they later came to be known). Some expressed a weariness with old imperial belief systems and sought to dislodge them. The majority, however, were not looking backward but forward. In modern evolutionary jargon, they were captivated by the lure of the future (explored in chapter 6).

It is this later group that baffles many conventional religionists and church figureheads, who tend to accuse those supporting the new spiritual awakening as rootless, reckless, and superficial (*postmodern* is the label often used). The critics miss the crucial breakthrough—one that is fueled by a lure from up ahead rather than a blatant disregard of sacred tradition. The Spirit who blows where she wills is spearheading a new awakening that defies not just one but several of the normalizing forces of earlier times.

Life Stages

Psychology too had its midcentury revolution. Beyond the psychodynamic vision of Sigmund Freud and the behaviorist philosophy of B. F. Skinner, evolutionary consciousness paved the way for a more insightful analysis of developmental growth throughout the entire human life-span. Psychology itself became suspicious of the emphasis on late adolescence as the peak of developmental growth and the formation of human character. The notion of *life stages* came on to the agenda and would play a leading role in the closing decades of the twentieth century.

Erik H. Erikson (1902–1994) became another guru of the late twentieth century. Interestingly, one of his key works, *Identity and the Life Cycle* was also published in 1959. Although still interested primarily in childhood and adolescence, Erikson extended the possibility of character formation and psychological growth into later adult phases of the young adult, mid-life, and old age. The following is his outline of life stages:

1. *Hope: Trust vs. Mistrust* (Oral-sensory, Birth to 2 years)
2. *Will: Autonomy vs. Shame and Doubt* (Muscular-Anal, 2–4 years)
3. *Purpose: Initiative vs. Guilt* (Locomotor-Genital, Preschool, 4–5 years)
4. *Competence: Industry vs. Inferiority* (Latency, 5–12 years)
5. *Fidelity: Identity vs. Role Confusion* (Adolescence, 13–19 years)

6. *Love: Intimacy vs. Isolation* (Young adulthood, 20–24, or 20–40 years)
7. *Care: Generativity vs. Stagnation* (Middle adulthood, 25–64, or 40–64 years)
8. *Wisdom: Ego Integrity vs. Despair* (Late adulthood, 65 to death)

His eight-stage structure became the basis of several other extended views, including that of James Fowler, an American, best known for his *Stages of Faith* (1981), which I reviewed extensively in my book *Adult Faith* (O'Murchu 2010, 112–16).

Fowler focuses much more explicitly on the adult phases of the life cycle. He believes that an adult appropriation of faith is unlikely to happen before the young adult stage (20–35), and in most cases will not transpire till mid-life (35–55), often accompanied by a life-crisis, as succinctly argued by Richard Rohr (2011). Fowler's richest insight, in my opinion, is that of his analysis of old age, which he defines from sixty-five years onward. This phase tends to be subdivided by subsequent reviewers of Fowler's work, for example, Mary Catherine Bateson (2010), Bill Plotkin (2008), and Diarmuid O'Murchu (2010).

New Adult Crisis Situations

Currently in the United States, a great deal of research is focused on the process of *emerging adulthood*. In developmental terms, when does a person make the transition from the pre-adult (adolescent) and appropriate an adult value system? Writing in the late 1990s, Jeffrey J. Arnett (2000) identified this stage in the age bracket of eighteen to twenty-five. Smith and Snell (2009) opt for eighteen to twenty-nine, whereas I myself tend to favor the age range of twenty-five to thirty-five. What is noteworthy in most of this research is a tendency not to name it as the stage of the *young adult,* since observation indicates high levels of fluidity and a strong experiential sense of being in transition for many people in their twenties and indeed right up till the age of forty.

Emerging adulthood (rather than young adult) is the description most frequently adopted, and as Smith and Snell (2009) indicate, faith appropriation at this stage is full of uncertainties, questions, and transitional restlessness. There are cultural differences that thus far seem to have been poorly researched. For instance, in emerging adulthood, while a sizable portion of Americans engage with faith matters, the majority of Europeans opt for something more akin to an agnostic stance. Europeans seem to be postponing the religious questions until they come to terms with the pressing interpersonal, social, domestic, and financial issues in a fluid and unpredictable market situation.

The kind of fluidity currently characterizing emerging adulthood sounds somewhat similar to what we used to associate with mid-life. Now *mid-life*—at least in the forties—seems to be a time of settling down, coming to terms with a world where some or many earlier dreams will never be fulfilled. The test of a fruitful mid-life now seems to be judged by the ability to make a range of adjustments resulting in a set of "good-enough" outcomes that provide some guarantee that life is worth living and that one is making a reasonable contribution to building a better future—for oneself and for the surrounding culture.

What still remains central to the mid-life breakthroughs is the ability to take one's cues from *internal wisdom* rather than external success. A great deal can still be achieved in terms of external accomplishment, but the underlying motivation—the wisdom that holds life together in a context of coherent meaning—is fueled from within, rather than from without. Commitment to key values along with a spiritual practice (not always clearly defined) tend to be regular features of the wisdom from within. Special friendships also play a central role. Church allegiance tends not to feature for the average European, but this seems to vary significantly in other parts of the world.

Another complex phase in contemporary human development is that of the fifties age-group. Throughout the closing decades of the twentieth century many people in the West entered their fifties with the prospect of an early retirement—from fifty-five onward—accompanied by a lucrative sum of money and several opportunities to explore other life experiences unavailable under the burden of earlier commitments. As we enter the twenty-first century, that scenario has changed dramatically. Early retirement is now discouraged, while layoffs are all too common (often without the lucrative payouts of just a few years ago). Moreover, people who chose to stay on till their early sixties and look forward to a substantial pension are now compelled to work till sixty-seven—often with a significantly reduced pension. And even in the so-called developed countries of the West, people in their fifties (and sixties) sometimes have to continue working to support their adult offspring who have lost jobs or become the victims of layoffs.

These new financial and social pressures tend to affect negatively the faith development of those in their fifties, also depleting their chances of sharing in the universalist spiritual vision highlighted by James Fowler and others (described below). Burdened by daily demands of trying to make ends meet and caring for significant others adversely affected by current economic pressures, people in their fifties tend to neglect their spiritual growth, or fulfill it by just going along with conventional church practice in the hope that it will gain them heavenly reward in a life hereafter. These people simply don't have the time or the energy to be worrying about religious matters. Religion seems largely irrelevant to their plight.

Growing Old Gracefully

As people live longer—even in poorer parts of the world—the time frame for old age has shifted from sixty-plus to seventy-plus. This is partly owing to demographic shifts in which elderly people now constitute a significant proportion of the world population, especially in Western nations. By the year 2020, we will have more people on the planet over the age of sixty than under the age of sixteen for the first time ever. Governments have been aware of this development, and the United Nations has carried out a number of major surveys. Political and economic strategists suspect that the rise of this new human subgroup may have a strong affect on several aspects of culture and lifestyle, yet few analysts offer clear indicators of what might lie ahead.

The chief barrier to an honest and insightful appraisal is probably the insidious power of prevailing attitudes. Throughout much of the modern world, old age tends to be viewed in a negative light. Old people are deemed to be productively useless and financially a burden on state resources, both of which are false and unjust allegations. In Western countries, older people contribute significantly to cultural and educational pursuits and often remain quite healthy even into advanced years. In many parts of Asia, Africa, and Latin America, particularly in extended families, older people often play a major role in child-rearing and home maintenance.

However, the current aging of the human population will precipitate a crisis and an opportunity that is likely to cast old age in a radically new light. The late cultural historian Theodore Roszak ended his writing career with two impressive analyses of this new cultural upsurge (2001; 2009). Although his review is focused primarily on the United States, the reader can readily extrapolate insights with a wider application. What happens when the majority of voters are of older age, with a more discerning eye for authentic leadership qualities devoid of the personal gains that tend to be stronger among younger voters? What happens when the dominant consumer is an older person who judges products by aesthetic and practical worth, and is not carried away by the propaganda of salacious advertising? The central point is this: *Older people tend to be more discerning and discriminating, more sustainable in lifestyle, and often more holistically aware of the bigger and broader issues.* Their shopping habits tend to be different from the popularly driven consumption targeted by glitzy advertising. Moreover, older people are often more sensitive and perceptive to life's values, even when they don't follow a particular creed or religion.

Our popular culture grossly misjudges and underestimates the potential of the emerging elder culture. The wise elder is coming back to haunt us all, and as researchers such as Theodore Roszak indicate, it may be the elderly rather than our youth who will prove to be the saviors of civilization—as long as we keep in mind that it will be quite a different civilization from the one that sustains our capitalistic consumerist culture.

Already in the 1970s—long before the demographic elder shift became apparent—James Fowler was making claims for older spiritual wisdom that were both original and provocative. Assuming that people have negotiated earlier life stages in a good-enough way, Fowler postulated for the age group of those seventy and older a strong possibility of flourishing into an altruistic outlook, a sense of gratitude and contentment for what has been, an awakening curiosity in spiritual values (not necessarily in the religious sphere), and the appropriation of a cosmic vision, expansive, egalitarian, and inclusive of cultural diversity.

Obviously, Fowler was influenced by what has since been called *the university of the third age* in the United States, wherein postretirement people make a conscious choice to engage with further learning, expansive exploration of emerging contemporary wisdom, transdisciplinary research, spiritual renewal, and social activism (peace and justice). These interests arise, it seems, from a renewed awareness and desire to contribute constructively and proactively to the creation of a better world for all. Older people read a great deal, create sharing groups, and reflect critically on the big questions of the modern world.

I have had the good fortune of encountering many such people at conferences and workshops throughout Canada and the United States. And my experience confirms the enthusiasm and confidence with which commentators such as Theodore Roszak, Mary Catherine Bateson, and Bill Plotkin write about this new phenomenon. My hope is that this generation of wise elders can engage more interactively and contribute more proactively to the fresh spiritual challenges that confront all adults in the world and church of our time.

Adult Faith

Public media give extensive coverage to the religious pessimism of our time and to a few articulate voices representing the new atheism (e.g., Richard Dawkins and the late Christopher Hitchens). The evolving spiritual consciousness does not seem to be sensational enough to captivate similar interest. Indeed, many adults whom I have encountered, exploring new spiritual possibilities, are not interested in being media celebrities and tend to be quite critical of how public media portray life in general.

Ironically, neither are churches and mainline religions interested in the spiritual awakening. It is perceived to be a threat, or perhaps a distraction from what the churches consider to be centrally important issues. To comprehend the emerging spirituality—and particularly its impact on adults of our time—requires a more subtle quality of discernment. Some people are reluctant to speak about their internal spiritual awakening. Others fear being dragged back to a formal religion they have long outgrown. Others still consider spirituality (and religion) a largely private affair, not to be exposed, where it might prove offensive to colleagues or loved ones.

The more conscientious, for whom the questions keep persisting, will tend to seek out kindred spirits in networks or social gatherings, at retreat centers or special conferences. Others may attend a workshop or join with some friends in studying one or more works of a popular contemporary writer. Others, still coping with the pressures of daily life (family, work, mortgage, and so on), rely on their church, synagogue, or mosque to help make sense of what is transpiring for them, but they tend to pick and choose—often unsure what criteria they are adopting in doing that.

Our adult years can span from thirty to ninety, and sometimes beyond. As we move through the various developmental life stages, outlined briefly above, perceptions and attitudes also change. The impact on religious belief can vary considerably, but these are some of the features that have been noted in a range of different cultural contexts:

- disillusionment with God as a parent-like figure;
- growing disbelief in God as an old bearded man living above the sky;
- Disregard for all the inherited metaphysical divine attributes: omnipotence, omniscience, etc.;

- a growing sense of discomfort with God-language in general;
- an awakening suspicion that much of the religious emphasis on guilt, shame, sin, and divine judgment is a strategy to cow people into submission and obedience;
- a tendency to accommodate religion within one's social and political values—leading to either positive or negative outcomes;
- a growing perceptual conviction that holiness belongs to the here-and-now rather than the hereafter: sacredness is within creation, not outside it. Dualistic divisions between sacred and secular no longer make sense; understanding creation more deeply (e.g., via science) is a surer way to God than religion;
- a felt need to distinguish between spirituality and religion, the former being more generic and empowering than the latter;
- religion's past oppression of women, which evokes a suspicion that religion often colludes with violence—even to the extent of validating warfare and oppression at times;
- the pursuit of a faith environment devoid of the imperial baggage of the past and the exclusive sanctioning of patriarchal institutions;
- seeking more collaborative, holarchical structures for engaging with growth in faith, as in the emerging evolution of *networking* in recent times.

As one's religious outlook changes—through some or all of the above transitions—new questions arise, and the questions are often felt to be empowering rather than destructive of one's inner spiritual meaning. This is where the adult faith seeker might first experience a dilemma: "Do I try to get rid of these questions? Or do I allow them even more scope and ventilation?" A growing body of adults in our time feels they should work with this restlessness rather than try to suppress it. In time, such questioning adults are likely to adopt one or more of these attitudinal changes:

- a desire to outgrow parental patronizing, often misinterpreted as distrust of authority;
- greater trust in one's intuitive wisdom;
- seeking out kindred spirits to discern intuitive insight rather than turning to established religious authorities;
- greater reliance on peer wisdom, rather than turning to experts, religious or otherwise;
- a search for local peer-based groups—along the lines of Basic Ecclesial Communities (BECs)—connected with the church but not controlled by it;
- a desire to explore and experiment with empowering rituals;
- interest in other world religions, and occasionally involvement in their rituals or practices, e.g., Eastern forms of meditation;
- a tendency to emphasize values related to achieving justice and the adoption of life changes to integrate such values;

- an orientation toward enlarged vision, especially around creation, ecology, and right livelihood;
- a growing sense that adult spirituality has at its core value the establishment of empowering and liberating relationships: at the personal, interpersonal, social, planetary, and cosmic levels;
- a dawning realization that most of the meaningless suffering in the world is the result of wrong human interference, which needs to be rectified by more informed justice-based action rather than waiting in vain for redemptive divine intervention.

The evolving adult of our time is not antireligion. She just considers religion to be archaic and irrelevant, and yearns for a more viable and empowering alternative. And in this new endeavor the seeking is more important than the finding, the questions more engaging than official answers. Dialogue is probably the single biggest strategy being sought out by these new adult faith seekers. Correspondingly, any indication of clerical or hierarchical patronizing is likely to rapidly alienate them.

One area yet to receive due attention is that of ethics and morality, particularly in an age of extensive experimentation of organic life—human and nonhuman alike. Religious morality is widely perceived to be narrowly preoccupied with individual private behavior, particularly in the sexual realm, while weak and collusive on the outrageous violence, exploitation, power-brokering, and pernicious advertising that characterize our modern world. On all these issues, formal religion has little or no impact, leaving adults quite unsure where to look for guidance.

Some adults suggest that governments need to be much more directly involved in developing and implementing moral values for the future. The dilemma here is that many of those same adults acknowledge that secular governments are even more corrupt than the religions are, leaving us with a moral vacuum that, as yet, we don't know how to fill.

The Journey Forth

In the subsequent chapters of this book, I am striving to create a framework whereby adult-faith seekers will generate the confidence to stay with the questions, the wisdom to await the evolving wisdom, and gather with supportive others to dialogue on the urgent issues evoking our engagement at this time.

The burning questions of the future—whether in politics, religion, or economics—are unlikely to arise from our time-honored institutions. Wisdom from the ground up, rather than from the top down, is likely to dominate the consciousness of the twenty-first century. In that regard, the worldwide web will play a crucial role, as more and more people such as Julian Assange will investigate institutional corruption, followed by ever louder calls for transparency and illuminating truth.

In the past we invested heavily in youth and projected many utopian visions around our young people as the hope of the future. Not since the cultural revolts of the 1960s have we had notable contributions from youth (late teens or early twenties). The emphasis on youth can be quite misleading and often misplaced, since our young people both reflect and criticize the values inherited from their seniors. Adults play a significant role in the formation of youth—to a degree that neither youth itself wishes to acknowledge or our dominant culture is capable of appreciating.

As James Fowler (and several other developmental psychologists) indicates, the concept of adolescence no longer has a clear start or end point; in some cases it extends well into the twenties, and may surface afresh in the transitional crises of the mid-life years. In popular culture, youth is often portrayed as exhibiting a free-for-all mentality (often labeled postmodernism), especially in the fluidity and diversity of intimate relationships and in work practices, which largely have become temporary and contractual in nature. What media do not highlight is the widespread insecurity of the younger generations, ensuing both in widespread escapist behaviors (e.g., drugs and alcohol) and in alignment in substantial numbers with fundamentalist sects and cults. The younger generations are seeking some sense of purpose and meaning in a world that has become fragile and scary.

This is a cultural milieu ripe for wise elders to provide a sense of grounding for frightened young people, but also for a growing proportion of adults so addicted to the struggle for survival that they have neither time nor energy to nurture their inner source of meaning. In this chaotic time, with major institutions failing us all around and a growing sense of fear and insecurity confronting us at every turn, we need a mature wisdom to make sense of what is happening and to refocus our attention on enduring truths of evolution and faith, as illuminated in the creative endeavors of scholars such as Ilia Delio (2013) and Carter Phipps (2012).

From within this cultural breakdown a new evolutionary impetus is likely to arise. It is not a return to the established norms of the past, but a growing sense of how to navigate our complex and fluid global culture. In the past our guides would have been outstanding philosophers and political heroes, representing the patriarchal wisdom that is rapidly losing credibility. I suspect next time round it will be mystics and alternative thinkers—and people of adult maturity and wisdom are likely to be the catalysts to see us through this perilous but promising epoch.

For Personal/Group Reflection

- In your faith development as an adult, when did you first begin to question your traditional beliefs?
- Assisted by the reflections of this chapter, can you trace the path your questioning has led you along?
- Can you name or outline six key features of the faith that now sustains you as an adult?
- Have you successfully negotiated structures through which you can articulate and further develop your newly appropriated sense of adult faith?

- How successful have you been in networking with other adults exploring a similar spiritual search for meaning?
- Do you agree or disagree with the envisioned significance of older people in adult faith development of the future?

Chapter Two

Faith in God

The human person glimpses the mystery of God, not as absence, but as overabundance.

— Jeannine Hill Fletcher

Our unjust society and our perverted idea of God are in close and terrible alliance.

— Elizabeth A. Johnson

I am not sure why Jeremy sought out my friendship. He knew I was a religious believer and formally committed to my Catholic religion as a religious and a priest. On our very first meeting he told me he was an atheist. We were both first-year psychology students at university. I lived in the closet of conventional religion and felt distinctly uncomfortable with Jeremy's friendly overtures. I don't know why our friendship endured, but it did, and it became the basis of insights that have intrigued me ever since then.

What intrigued me more than anything else was Jeremy's paradoxical persistence: he never failed to assert his allegiance to atheism while he exhibited an unmistakable fascination with the reality of God. He used the word *God* more frequently than I did. And he was asking metaphysical questions, plummeting depths of mystery that baffled and confused me. To my own embarrassment I began to realize that he was wrestling with religious faith with a fervor that I could not match.

After one of our many conversations, and a friendship now quite solidly grounded, I began to realize that Jeremy's religious awakening echoed Blaise Pascal's oft-cited affirmation from God: "You would not be searching for me, except that you have already found me" (*Pensées*, 553). Jeremy was reluctant to agree but conceded that he was pursuing a search for meaning that was unlikely to have a solely human answer.

Purifying Religion

It was many months later before I read the research of the Latino scholar Antonio Pérez Esclarín (1978) who made the bold assertion that atheists should never be judged by their overt statements. Subconsciously, Pérez Esclarín asserted, atheists are not trying to deny or destroy God, but striving to rid religion of its superficiality and idolatry. And that is exactly what Jeremy was doing, although neither he nor I had realized it at the time.

In the contemporary world, religious indifference, rather than atheism, seems far more prevalent. People drift away from religion, to the point of sometimes abandoning all semblance of religious faith. Occasionally, a life crisis may reawaken religious sentiment, the outcome of which will often depend on what pastoral resources are available to help deal with the crisis.

Genuine atheists may be identified as those who chose to opt out of religion for reasons of conscientious objection. A frequent occurrence is that of the objection to the violence embedded within religion, as explored by Sam Harris (2005) and Jack Nelson-Pallmeyer (2003). The sincerity of such objection is all too apparent, but sadly formal religious leadership often fails to take note.

Contemporary adults, raising the burning questions explored in this book, often fear that they might be sliding into atheism, and this can worry them greatly. I hope Jeremy's story, with which I open this chapter, will reassure such seeking adults that so-called atheism can in fact be an important step, not merely to a more purified sense of faith, but to a more empowering spirituality.

Much more disquieting is the dark night of soul and senses that many spiritual seekers experience. This is not merely a stage in classical mystical awakening. Often it can feel like a total breakdown of religious sentiment and aspiration. Nothing from one's previous practice—meditation, prayer, reading, liturgy—seems to work anymore. God seems totally absent, and any attempt at reconnecting with mystery or meaning culminates in a spiritual black hole.

Spiritual accompaniment—with a good friend, soulmate, or spiritual director (in the more formal sense)—is recommended for people enduring such spiritual dryness of spirit. A formal process of accompaniment may do little to relieve the spiritual angst, but frequently it will serve as a catalyst for a breakthrough, major or minor. When the breakthrough eventually happens, it is often unexpected and surprising. What precisely brings it about, one may never be able to identify. Perhaps, it is a case of being surprised by the Christian notion of *grace*. Generally, the result is greater equanimity and peace, although doubts and questions may still exist.

Sometimes, it is the process of such a journey through the dark night that convinces one that authentic adult religion is all about doubt and question, a seeking that never ceases, a finding always postponed, or at best partially realized. Religionists are quick to condemn such fluidity as relativism, devoid of all truth and certainty. For adult seekers of our time, relativism is often viewed as a great protection against idolatry, the worship of false Gods, of which religion itself may be one of the most intractable.

Confronting Institutional Codependency

Which brings us to the complex question of codependency, a phenomenon briefly addressed in my book *Adult Faith* (2010, 24–25), and now requiring further elaboration. As commonly used, the word *codependency* applies to a set of behaviors indicating an unhealthy dependency arising from a dysfunctional network of relationships, as in a spousal alcoholic partnership, or in a family where issues of conflict are neither acknowledged nor confronted. In religious terms we encounter the additional expression of institutional codependency that can be recognized in behaviors such as excessive guilt, diminished self-worth, gullibility, willingness to be manipulated, and the need to be needed.

Another symptom of codependency is dishonesty and denial. Conventional Christians often lie to themselves about being happy with the denominational menu they are offered. They perpetuate the lie with their children and new converts because the pain of confronting the truth is too much. And so they continue to pass on to others, particularly to their offspring, doctrines and beliefs that they themselves no longer subscribe to (more in Hoffman 1991; also Crosby 1991 [2011]).

I will attempt to illustrate this subtle and disturbing issue by sharing a personal narrative of a long-time cherished friend. Suzanne is a lifelong practicing Catholic, whom I have known for almost forty years. Now in her late fifties, she is mother to five grown-up children and still works as a school administrator in her home country of Ireland. Suzanne is a university graduate with a degree in public administration. She is described by colleagues as a highly intelligent woman, caring, diligent, and very effective in her work. In fact, her school has been described as "a model for modern education."

In a conversation with Suzanne in February 2012, I asked how she felt about the new translation of the Catholic Mass (introduced in Ireland in December 2011). This was her response: *"I don't even think about it; I take it as it comes; I don't understand what it means and obviously I am not meant to understand."* Momentarily, I did not know what to say, and as Suzanne changed the topic of our conversation, I saw no point in returning to my original query.

Have you detected the point of my story? Here is a highly intelligent, competent, spiritually aware human being who seems to morph into something akin to an infantile state when it comes to the practice of her faith. I found her phrase, *"I am not meant to understand,"* particularly strange and disturbing. In no other sphere of her life is she likely to use this phrase, so what has happened in her religious development and formation that has locked her into this unreflective state?

Although I don't wish to sound unjustly judgmental, it looks as if Suzanne is locked into a serious form of codependency—in terms of her church allegiance and her internalization of faith. And she is not alone—I have met many adult people occupying this dysfunctional space. Fortunately, more people are awakening to what they have colluded with and are beginning to break loose from such dysfunctionality.

Formal religion in general is riddled with codependent elements, which can easily ensnare and delude even highly intelligent people like Suzanne. These are some of the features that feed the codependency:

1. A childhood indoctrination depicting God as a perfect and all powerful parental figure, thus consigning the devotee to the internalized status of a passive, dependent child (hence the phrase: children of God).
2. Childhood internalization of God as a demanding distant judge to whom we must one day render an account, with the threat of severe punishment.

3. To stay on good terms with this demanding deity, the devotee complies by fulfilling one's obligations to God—through the church.

4. Several patriarchal ploys are interwoven in this religious indoctrination, the primary one being subtle control, by continually reminding devotees of their dependency on religion, along with the dire consequences of not being faithful, reinforcing the lure into codependent allegiance.

5. Fear and unworthiness are assumed to be virtuous when in fact they are patriarchal ploys consigning people to a kind of naïve innocence, or strategies employed to evoke submission.

6. This quality of religion exerts a strong influence on, and appeal for, people who are materially poor, or living with much pain, suffering, or oppression. When conditions improve, people begin to lapse in their allegiance.

7. Such religiosity is often couched in a language that tends to give regal glory to the all-powerful God, while demanding of powerless humans a perpetual state of repentance. The language also tends to be heavily dualistic, dismissive of the natural world, and focused on fulfillment in a life hereafter—all features of the new Catholic translation of the Roman missal.

8. Such is the virulence of this indoctrination, that even people with advanced educational qualifications, and particularly those entrusted with parental responsibilities, can be lured into an

unreflective and naïve acceptance of a religiosity that is clearly incongruent with the sense of
adulthood they readily assume in so many other
areas of their lives.

Fortunately, in our time, more and more adults are
recognizing the false allurement of such religiosity and are
beginning to deal with it in a discerning, adult manner.
Some opt out completely in the hope of making a fresh
start, a noble aspiration that is dauntingly difficult to
negotiate as there are so few alternatives. Many remain
loosely attached and hope to activate changes from within
the system that will engage and embrace their newly dis-
covered sense of adult faith; this usually proves much
more challenging than initially envisaged. Conflict with
clergypersons or with diocesan structures present recurring obstacles; in several cases the ecclesiastic structures
do not seem congenial to the awakening of adult faith. As
Michael Crosby (1991) highlights, it is the system itself
that is fundamentally dysfunctional, a problem we will re-
visit in chapter 5.

Around the Christian world and from the Catholic
Church in particular, millions have walked away—either
in protest or in disillusionment. Perhaps this was the rebellious catharsis necessary—the clearing out—that had to
happen before the reappropriation of the adult could com-
mence. After the dissolution of an unworkable marriage,
people often need to take space and distance before consid-
ering a new commitment. In the case of a fresh commitment
to religion or church, the issues are considerably complex

and require a quality of pastoral resourcefulness largely unknown in the church today.

I hope that the reflections of this book will provide
some important elements for both context and resourcefulness, the issues that need to be highlighted in terms of the
painful letting go, the transitional processes that need to
be identified and established, and how best to discern and
befriend alternative options that will need to be brought to
birth for a more adult church of the future—a topic further
explored in chapter 6 below.

Birthing the Adult Believer

Adult faith in the twenty-first century is not merely a pursuit of clarification. It is much more about a new cultural
awakening seeking to honor complexity, diversity, and mystery. Simplistic answers aimed at religious or moral compli-
ance may have some relevance for children and younger
people, but they are not appropriate for adults and most
likely will generate cynicism and negative reaction rather
than an awakening of authentic faith. And there is no subject
that cannot be questioned—even the mystery of God itself.
The awakening of an adult quality of faith nearly always
involves—to one degree or another—a break with inherited
beliefs. Rarely does it evolve into what might be labeled
full-blown atheism (whatever exactly that is). Adults tend
to go through a process with well-defined stages.

1. *Inner Questioning.* This questioning is a kind of
   gut reaction, seeking clarification around things
   a priest or pastor might have said, a ritual that

feels empty rather than inspiring, a moral guide-
line of questionable worth. The inner questioning intermingles with a sensitive conscience,
characterized by hesitancy to question matters
that one would not dare to have questioned ten
years previously.

2. *Substantial doubts.* For educated Westerners,
    questions about the possibility of Gospel mira-
    cles, the virgin birth, or the Resurrection of Je-
    sus quite frequently surface.

3. *Cynicism.* This often arises when there is no ob-
    vious forum in which serious doubts can be ex-
    plored and talked through in a supportive and
    nonjudgmental space.

4. *Drifting.* Regular church attendance begins to
    wane—and with less guilt as time transpires.
    This may deepen the quest for more authen-
    tic spirituality or may lead into a vague kind
    of agnosticism. We note this in Christians who
    will participate in church services for funerals,
    weddings, and christenings and may attend
    church services at special times, such as Christ-
    mas, but otherwise, they just drift further and
    further away.

5. *Challenge.* A person develops sufficient self-
    confidence to challenge a clergyperson or church
    authority on a matter of official teaching or sac-
    ramental practice. If the challenge is accepted
    and there is an openness to explore it further,
    these people will continue to engage in that pro-
    cess. If they meet with rebuff—especially at an

early stage—they may quickly break off the connection and begin exploring serious alternatives.
It is in this realm that we often hear people dis-
tinguishing *religion* from *spirituality.*

6. *Attempting serious change.* Faith becomes a serious life issue; the seeker wishes to be taken
seriously and not fobbed off by conventional
creedal statements or standard church practice.
This is where the adult faith seeker comes into
his or her own. In the pastoral domain it is very
much virgin territory.

7. *Exploring alternatives.* Because we live in an age
of mass information, human curiosity has been
awakened to levels largely unknown to previous generations. People enjoy diversity, and it
begins to feel more congruent and credible than
monolithic truth. Adults become suspicious of
any system—religious or secular—that clings to
one dominant mode of thought or praxis. The
universe is perceived to be too vast and complex for what is considered to be naïve simplic-
ity. Adults embrace diversity, to a degree that
feels threatening to the wider culture of the traditional church, often leaving the explorer on a
lonely journey, often unsure where to turn next.

Faith and Belief

To understand what is transpiring for the adult seeker
we need to distinguish between faith and its articulation
through various belief systems and their respective doctrines.

Traditionally, faith is understood as a gift divinely bestowed: you either have it or you don't, and only God's grace can make it possible for you. Once you have it, you protect and develop it by allegiance to the formal beliefs propounded by a particular Christian denomination or a world religion. According to the traditional view, those doctrines never change; faith therefore is a matter of accepting them or rejecting them. If you do accept and faithfully follow the rules, then you stand a good chance of being saved; if you are not faithful, you are likely to suffer the consequences in a life hereafter.

For adults of our time, the chasm between belief and faith grows larger by the day. Millions of adults—and young people as well—do not take religion seriously. It strikes them as archaic and irrelevant, and not worth all the hassle that ensues. For others, they are loath to let go of something that has been important in the past, and still carries significance, but intuitively they know that such significance is waning, and they don't know quite what to do about it. For such people church life and teaching carry decreasing import, and yet they consider it important to christen their children, have religious funerals, and attend church for special feasts such as Christmas and Easter.

On the face of it, it would seem that the majority of one-time religious adherents are either drifting or making convenient accommodation for that which still carries some meaning for them. This group is so vast and diffuse that it is impossible to conduct sociological surveys to establish dominant trends—the trends themselves change at an ever more rapid rate. My interest in the present work are people of *adult life stages* who have a renewed interest in religious matters and are seeking forums of engagement more congruent with their adult questions and explorations.

The God Word

Those seeking to appropriate a more adult faith tend to feel uneasy about the word *God*. It carries so much baggage from the past, particularly associations with a distant king-like ruler, dictating and controlling everything from a faraway heavenly realm, a judgmental figure always on the lookout to reprimand and punish wayward humans. An authoritarian figurehead requiring dominant males on earth through whom God communicates and implements God's desire for absolute control. An anthropocentric creature primarily concerned about human superiority, with little interest in the material creation, deemed to be merely a resource for human usufruct.

No doubt, several readers will object: "But that is not the God that I believe in," suggesting that our understanding of God has changed, and will change, with the evolution of time and culture. Yet when theologians formally acknowledge this change and seek to work out its implications, they are often castigated and even denounced by church authorities. Which leads to a further observation: *The understanding of God among the believing masses is much more fluid and flexible than the views often held by official churches and religions.* For the latter, the priority of God is indisputable and a necessary requirement for the maintenance of patriarchal religion.

For adult faith seekers of our time, there are those of lateral vision and perception who are not too worried about the God-word; they wear it lightly, deeming it to be a linguistic term denoting a great deal more than any one word could embody. There are others desiring the abolition of the word and suggesting replacements like: *Source of Our Being, Holy Mystery, the Holy One, Great Spirit.* The desire seems to be to transcend the anthropocentric reductionism (God as a superior human person) and rediscover the ubiquity of holy mystery in the entire cosmic-planetary web of creation.

The presence of divine mystery throughout creation serving as a focus for human faith is not as original as we may initially think. The great theologian and doctor of the church, Saint Thomas Aquinas, seems to have been endorsing this view when he wrote: "If we don't understand creation correctly, we can't hope to understand God correctly" (Aquinas 1956) Aquinas's statement is an insight adopted by some modern scholars who propose that creation itself is God's primary revelation for us (see Christie 2013). In other words, the first and oldest evidence for God at work is in the evolution of creation itself.

However, it is precisely the conviction of God's involvement in creation that begins to problematize the God-word itself. Scientifically and spiritually, we are moving away from the idea of creation as an organism that requires a prime mover and still requires a prime sustainer. Divine empowering mystery is itself inherent in creation's growth and development. Too quickly, fundamentalists label this insight as *pantheism*, pronouncing God as nothing more than the creation itself. In these observations I am not speculating about God—but seeking to contemplate and explore the divine at work in creation, using creation itself as the primary raw material in which we humans glimpse Holy Mystery at work.

This is where we connect with the contemporary adult seeker, often suspicious of how Christian theologians try to control God and project onto God a range of human projections, particularly related to power and domination. Reflective adults today feel more at ease not seeking to explain every dynamic at work in the divine life. In a way similar to that of Buddhists, such adults say: "Let God be God; our task is to make the world a more God-like place by getting rid of meaningless suffering."

To traditional believers this sounds like agnosticism out and out. It is a great deal more subtle than that. We are dealing with a type of mystical intuition, endowed with a strong resistance against any human attempt at controlling God. It seeks a radical transparency to the mysterious unfolding of the creative universe, with the underlying conviction (often poorly articulated) that Holy Mystery breaks out and breaks through in the evolutionary unfolding of universal life. Our human task is not to speculate about this God but to co-create its dynamic unfolding.

To traditional believers, it sounds like a rather impersonal God and therefore verging on paganism or idolatry. Dualistic splitting plays a significant role here. If something cannot be called *personal*—as understood anthropocentrically—then it must be *impersonal*. As I suggest elsewhere (O'Murchu 2011, 42–55; 2012, 183–93), we break through the dualism by adopting the notion of the *transpersonal* (more on pp. 66–69 below). Meanwhile, some adults veer more in the direction of process theology (Keller 2003; 2008); they view God as an inherent dimension of the evolving universe, with a particular significance (as something akin to a human person) and a universal connotation, which sounds rather impersonal but in fact is the creative foundation for all forms of becoming—including that of human personhood.

The Trinitarian Construct

In childhood catechesis, contemporary adults were told either that the Trinity is a mystery that they really are not meant to understand, or they were invited into an intellectual quagmire of trying to fit three into one, which in all probability left them baffled and confused. For adult faith seekers, the notion of the Trinity is either a concept of no consequence (many never even think about it), or it is a spiritual insight that carries quite a profound meaning, especially in the light of theological developments throughout the closing decades of the twentieth century.

The theologian Elizabeth Johnson (2007, 202–25) provides a fine overview that several adult faith seekers find both enlightening and reassuring. In scanning the theological writings on the meaning of the Trinity across recent decades, she highlights the heavy emphasis on the relational dynamics that constitute the reality that we call God. In other words, the doctrine of the Trinity is a human attempt to name and explain a long-held spiritual conviction of the human spirit, namely that whatever else we discern about the divine mystery, above all it embodies a deep capacity for intimate relating. And this fundamental quality of the Godhead imbues everything in God's creation. Relationship, and not estrangement or isolation, is our default position in the divine plan, whether understood interpersonally or in planetary/cosmic terms.

For contemporary adult seekers, it is also reassuring and inspiring to note that a doctrine of the Trinity exists in every major faith system known to humankind. In the case of Judaism and Islam, we find it in their mystical branches, the Kabbalah and Sufism, respectively. Despite all the cultural and political differences, the religions hold this one truth in common: God—by whatever name we use—represents a fundamental orientation to everything in creation, including the divinity itself, namely the capacity for deep bonding. This—and not all the emphasis on sin, flaw, and corruption—is where religion should begin in its attempts to connect humanity to the divine source. The power of love is the center of our existence and the rationale for everything in creation, the divine life included. (For more see Zizioulas 2006; Polkinghorne 2010.)

Adult Faith-Becoming

When it comes to belief in divine reality, the following seem to be the crucial issues that adults wrestle with:

- Anthropocentric constructs of divine life tend to confuse and bewilder contemporary adults. Imaging God as a transcendent human-like figure, whether as Father or Son, does not ring true anymore; in fact, it alienates rather than inspires.
- Adults today don't seem to have the same spiritual need for the "personal" God deemed to be essential by formal religionists. The notion of a

personal God seems to be ensnared in anthropocentric projections that lead to codependency
rather than authentic human life.

- The codependency translates into needing a
  heavenly parent, who will tell us what we should
  do. This codependency in adult faith seekers
  is replaced with the spiritual discernment and
  maturation that arises from adult mutuality
  where two or three are gathered in God's name.

- The patriarchal tenor of so much inherited religion is quite alien to many contemporary adult
  faith seekers.

- The violence that is embedded in many religious
  systems, as in the Christian theories of redemption, is a feature of religion adults wish to get
  rid of.

- Adults are moving away from the notion of wor-
  shipping God, the divine idol above or beyond.
  The language of co-creating with the divine life-
  force exercises a deeper appeal. Ritual (as dis-
  tinct from conventional worship) seeks to engage
  and celebrate the divine will-to-meaning at work
  throughout the creation.

- Adults find the God they discover through creation's unfolding to be more real and empowering than the God(s) envisaged in the formal
  religions.

- Adults warm to the notion of a divine life-force
  endowed with a deep capacity for bonding, inviting all creatures in the matrix of creation into

a grand collaborative endeavor, one that none-theless honors the great paradox of creation and destruction so necessary for evolutionary creativity—precisely how indigenous peoples understand the role of the Great Spirit (more in O'Murchu 2012).

- For Christians desiring a different sense of en-gagement with divine reality, Jesus serves as an empowering model. However, the understand-ing of Jesus is also significantly different from the conventional portrayal—as I indicate in the next chapter.

Orthopraxy Rather Than Orthodoxy

Contemporary adult faith seekers tend to be suspicious of religious dogmas, Christian and otherwise. They experi-ence the anthropocentric flavor as a form of reductionism that diminishes the elegance of holy mystery and even un-dermines human mystery. Adults yearn for an experiential grounding whereby they can engage directly and creatively with the sacredness they detect within the fabric of creation itself, a sacredness now illuminated by several insights of modern science and cosmology.

Adults believe that we live within a mystery that is holy and profound, one that encapsulates the entire web of life, planetary and cosmic. And they feel the deep pain of religious cultures that seem incapable of apprehending this mystery in a direct and proactive way, as well as the many secular forces (monetary and political) that exploit and desecrate the creation we inhabit. For such adults the

God-inspired challenges of our time are not about right doctrine (orthodoxy) but about right praxis (orthopraxy).

At this juncture Christianity exerts a deep appeal, with its central notion of the Kingdom of God and the empowering relational dynamics involved therein. To that subject we turn our attention in the next chapter.

For Personal/Group Reflection

- How have you coped with religious codependency—in your own life and among your acquaintances?
- How helpful/unhelpful do you find the need to image the Holy One?
- Some people do not like the word "God." What might we replace it with?
- Have you ever had mystical experiences? How have they contributed to your spiritual development?
- How comfortable do you feel with the notion of finding God in the heart of creation? How would you describe such a God?
- What parallels do you detect between the modern understanding of God as Trinity and the sense of the divine that arises in the New Cosmology?

Chapter Three

Faith in Jesus

We Christians need to begin again from Christ, from the contemplation of the one who has revealed in his ministry the plenitude of the fulfilment of the human vocation and its meaning.

— Bishop Demetrio Valentini,
Diocese of Jales, Brazil (2007)

[Jesus is] proposing a total meltdown and recasting of human consciousness, bursting through tiny acorn-selfhood—that we arrived on the planet with—into the oak tree of our fully realized personhood.

— Cynthia Bourgeault

Jesus continues to fascinate contemporary human beings. Ever since the mid-twentieth century, study of the historical Jesus, and of the faith tradition associated with him, has expanded exponentially. A great deal of this research adopts a critical analysis of what we claim to be the foundational truths of the Christian narrative. Virtually every dimension of the Jesus story has been critically reevaluated, and every major criticism claims to be based on substantial evidence. The following are some of the varying outcomes:

1. Jesus founded a new religion (namely Gentile-based Christianity) because the Jewish people—due to hardness of heart—refused the invitation to divine reform.
2. Jesus was sent by God to save humanity from its sinfulness and obtained our salvation by dying on the Cross for us.
3. Jesus founded the church, and fidelity to the church and its teachings is the task of Christian discipleship, in fact, the only guarantee of obtaining the salvation Jesus wrought on our behalf.
4. Jesus was an eschatological prophet, seeking a fuller realization of Jewish messianism focused on a new heaven and a new earth. His true historical context is Judaism, not Christianity.
5. Jesus is a historical figure, but we know virtually nothing about his historical existence. Christian discipleship is a matter of faith, not of history (Rudolf Bultmann). The Gospels are largely leg-

endary tales, capable of generating faith, but unreliable as historical documents.

6. Jesus was a Jewish prophet, seeking the reform of Judaism. He never intended a new religion in his name (Vermès 1973; Sanders 1985; Casey 2010).

7. Jesus sought the end of all formal religion, inviting and challenging people to engage creatively with the call to live fully in our engagement with God's creation (Sheehan 1986).

8. The historical Jesus never actually existed (Harpur 2004). He serves as an archetype embodying ideal human aspirations—similar to other legendary figures such as the Egyptian Horus, the Greek Dionysius, the Hindu Krishna.

9. Even if the historical Jesus did exist, his existence should be understood primarily as that of an archetypal figure, representing human ideals to which all humans aspire (Childs 2000; Wink 2002). He therefore commands an enduring and irresistible fascination, enriched by his historical existence, but not dependent on it.

10. For Christians, Jesus embodies a high point of human evolutionary achievement, in addition to providing the lure for our future evolutionary growth (O'Murchu 2008). Other archetypal figures serve a similar purpose in the other great religions, for example, the avatars of Hinduism and the bodhisattvas in Buddhism (O'Murchu 2008, 144ff.).

Such a rich and complex mélange! How does the Christian seeker of our time make sense of it all? More important for this book, how does the adult explorer embrace this complex landscape and from it distill a viable and vibrant faith for the twenty-first century?

The Conventional Picture

For the vast majority of conventional Christians positions 1–3 above capture the central significance of their Christian belief. Jesus is a historical person sent by God to save sinners, a process of redemption that now continues through the life and practice of the Christian church. It is precisely this same stance that adult faith seekers revolt against. Adults see this construct as too narrowly anthropocentric, guilt-ridden, codependent, and disempowering for those who interpret religious belief as an invitation into co-creative collaboration with the divine presence at work in the whole of creation.

This is not how the majority of Christians see their call to faith. In this book, therefore, I am dealing with a Christian minority, but one that is gaining cultural and religious significance in the modern world. Much more serious is the quality of commitment characterizing the two groups. Sociologically, we know that the biggest drop-off in religious practice is from the majority group, those who gradually drift away rather than make a conscientious choice to stop practicing. The minority, however—those described as adult faith seekers in this book—tend to be the ones who choose to remain faithful, reworking their inherited wisdom, seeking to reform the formal church both from within and without; they increasingly provide an informed critique of a church that they feel has lost its way amid the plethora of historical contingencies or unexamined allegiance to ideologies such as patriarchal domination.

Adults belonging to the Christian faith seek to engage with a double dynamic. First, they wish to dislodge the historical baggage that prevents the church from engaging in an adult way with past and present issues. Second, they use creativity and imagination to mine afresh the scriptural tradition to empower more innovative channels for faith articulation in the future. The first part of this chapter outlines briefly the inherited baggage perceived to be a hindrance to present and future growth.

The language and imagery adopted by both the Scriptures and liturgical worship raise several concerns for people who wish to adopt an adult stance. Inundated with references to patriarchal power and a substantial amount of violent rhetoric, such literary constructs not only alienate adult Christians but also strike them as being spiritually and theologically bankrupt. Let's briefly look at a popular psalm and a hymn still currently used in Christian worship.

A passage from Psalm 117 reads as follows:

> The nations all encompassed me; in the Lord's name
> I crushed them.
> They encompassed me about like bees; they blazed
> like a fire among thorns.
> In the Lord's name I crushed them.
> I was hard-pressed and was falling, but the Lord
> came to help me.

The Lord is my strength and my song; he is my
    savior. . . .
The Lord's right hand has triumphed; his right has
    raised me.
The Lord's right hand has triumphed.
I shall not die, I shall live and recount his deeds.
I was punished; I was punished by the Lord, but
    not doomed to die.

It seems that many such psalms were originally written to
sustain people in the midst of terrible suffering, and the praying of such psalms would certainly evoke hope and a resolve
to persevere. Undoubtedly, they can still evoke meaning for
contemporary peoples living in oppressive conditions, but for
a growing body of adults—even in adverse circumstances
—the impact of such spirituality is becoming increasingly
problematic.

In my book *Adult Faith* (O'Murchu 2010, 68–69), I
highlight the distinction between *the devotion of consolation*
and *the spirituality of liberation*. In our discernment of adult
faith for our time, we are employing a critically important
distinction. The passage from Psalm 117 expresses quite vividly the devotion of consolation: crushed and disempowered
people are encouraged to look to the God of might and tri-
umph to rescue them from their oppressive plight. God is all-
powerful, and the people are passively powerless. The people
are totally dependent on the One who holds the liberating
power.

This dualistic split between power and powerlessness is
the basis of the disempowering codependency that adults of
our time seek to outgrow. In the spirituality of liberation, peo-

ple reclaim the right to empowerment by mutually mobilizing their collective resourcefulness, to co-create with God, rather than passively submit to a sense of divine power described in the language of dualistic splitting and patriarchal power projections. The Gospel vision of the Companionship of Empowerment (kingdom of God) seeks to transcend all forms of patriarchal codependency, requiring us to interpret afresh the message and language of all Christian prayer, the psalms included.

Christian hymnology faces an even more daunting hermeneutical reform. Many of our popular hymns are couched in the language of regal power and glory, sometimes incorporating a cult of victimhood as part of the submission to divine royal power. We detect this disturbing combination in the following Christian hymn:

> Christ triumphant ever-reigning, Savior, Master, King.
> Lord of heav'n, our lives sustaining, hear us as we sing:
> Yours the glory and the crown, the high renown,
> the eternal name.
> Suffering servant, scorned, ill-treated, victim
> crucified!
> Death is through the Cross defeated, sinners justified.

Echoes of atonement theology reverberate throughout this passage. The titles of *Savior, Master, King* were liberally used by Roman emperors, for example, Caesar Augustus. It seems that Jesus in proclaiming the Companionship of Empowerment totally denounced kingship in all its imperial content, so why do we hold on to it so explicitly in our Christian

hymnology? Paradoxically, this powerful kinglike God becomes the victim for redemptive rescue. Death itself is de-
monized instead of being viewed as an integral and essential
dimension of all life processes, personal and planetary alike.
And passive sinful creatures are reconciled with the suffering
imperial Lord.

Within the Christian community today are those who
unquestioningly accept this devotional construct, and many
seek it out in the hope of surviving and making some sense
out of their awful anguish and suffering. But there is a
growing body of contemporary adults who are alienated
by this kind of religious rhetoric. It depicts a view of God
and humans at variance with their incarnational awakening and the contemporary call to work collaboratively and
creatively within the Companionship of Empowerment.

Adult faith seekers today face a formidable task of discernment. What quality of Christian discipleship are we
called to embrace? And in striving to respond in adult ways
how do we reintegrate our inherited sense of faith with so
much baggage related to patriarchal power, human and
earthly disempowerment, and the rhetoric of atonement,
questioned in recent times by a growing group of contemporary theologians? In moving from such a problematic
past, adults will need to engage with paradoxical and even
contradictory elements, particularly this oft-cited set of
convictions:

1. *Jesus is the Redeemer of the World.* Creation, due
   to some strange, inexplicable divine arrange-
   ment, is flawed and sinful, and can only be set

right by a once-off divine intervention. God sent
Jesus to rescue humanity from this sinful world,
through the mediation provided by the church.
People believe in Jesus and follow him in order
to be saved.

2. A variation of No. 1: *The Pentecostal Position.*
   Salvation is achieved by the historical Jesus but
   carried out—via the church—mainly by the
   Holy Spirit.

3. *Jesus is the primary model of true holiness.* In
   the world there is an irredeemable conflict between the sacred and the secular. Jesus is the
   way of the sacred and the surest guide to its full-
   est realization. Holiness alone enables us to live
   meaningfully in this world and, at the end of
   life, find salvation in a world beyond. This view
   is widely adopted by Catholics particularly.

4. *Christian faith creates rather than solves problems.* With so much emphasis on guilt and spiritual escapism, allegiance to Christianity can become a distraction from serious commitment to
   making the world a better place. Consequently,
   adults often conclude: "It is not worth all the
   hassle. Let's leave it to one side, and perhaps use
   it occasionally (e.g., at funerals)." This may be
   described as the postmodern or agnostic position, and has been growing rapidly in the opening decades of the twenty-first. century.

5. *Jesus is the primary disciple of the Kingdom of
   God* seeking an earthly (eschatological) trans-

formation in which justice, love, nonviolence, and healing become the key elements aimed at something akin to heaven on earth. The church can be a catalyst to bring about such transformation, but the enterprise is bigger and broader than the church. This view—evolving mainly in the latter half of the twentieth century—is espoused by probably *no more than 10 percent* of the worldwide Christian community, and tends to viewed suspiciously by church authorities.

In the above list, the reader can easily detect the common elements in the first four positions: human dependency on the redemptive powerful God, with the Cross as a central symbol (even when it is linked with Resurrection). Position 5 moves us on to a very different level. It characterizes a shift toward empowerment, the foundations for the co-creative collaboration that inspires and engages adult people of faith today. Its dynamics and implications are the focus of the reflections for the remainder of this chapter.

What Inspires the Christian Adult?

There is an enormous potential in the Christian faith for adult engagement, and the historical Jesus carries an enduring fascination for many spiritual seekers of our time. Some adults support the conviction of some contemporary scholars that Jesus was about the reform of Judaism rather than the founder of a new religion. Jesus as a prophetic-type reformer, seeking to make his religion more relevant and empowering for a culture of justice and right living, certainly has a contemporary adult appeal.

Adult believers, however, seem to be even more attracted to that which they perceive to be something radically
new in the message and life witness of Jesus. The Gospels
name this new feature as the *Kingdom of God* (with scholars endlessly debating the degree to which it is new). The
phrase is a direct translation from Greek, the language in
which the Gospels were written. In the 1970s, Christian
scholars devoted considerable attention to the Jewish background of the historical Jesus, noting that in his preaching and teaching Jesus would have used Aramaic, and not
Greek, the language through which we access the teaching
of the Gospels today.

Greek is a written language, the meaning of which is
judged primarily through what we see on the written page,
but Aramaic was a spoken language, the meaning of which
is judged primarily by sound and not by sight. Two
thousand years later it is impossible to recover the precise
meanings Jesus would have conveyed through the Aramaic
idiom—and scholars seem reluctant to probe too deeply—
but it certainly would have been different from the more
precise literary structure of the Greek. Aramaic is considered to embody a much more ornate, elaborate, and poetic
set of meanings, which may have been neglected or even
undermined in the Greek rendering of the Gospels.

The Aramaic word for "kingdom" is *Malkuta*, with distinctive connotations of mutual empowerment rather than
exerting power over. In an attempt to honor the primacy of
the Aramaic, some scholars suggest a more empowering ren-
dition, namely that of the *Companionship of Empowerment*.
Apart from the linguistic details (which preoccupy scholars),
the merit of this translation is that it opens up a range of

Christian meanings more congruent with the parables and the several empowering strategies adopted by the historical Jesus in his preaching and befriending of the oppressed, the poor, and the marginalized.

This kind of language resonates deeply with adult faith seekers today. Conscious of inhabiting a world where millions are disempowered by poverty, oppression, exploitation, violence, and injustice, these emerging adults want a faith system that embraces the notion of empowerment in a real and authentic way. They detect in the life praxis of the historical Jesus one who took the empowerment with ultra-seriousness, challenging oppressive structures forthrightly and courageously, even to the point that it cost him his life. For the contemporary adult seeker today, such "salvation" is not grounded in the death of Jesus but primarily in the experience and inspiration of his daily life.

The notion of *companionship* also resonates deeply. So complex are the major economic, political, and social issues of our time that individuals on their own are hopelessly outdone in trying to rectify the injustices. It requires collective endeavor, with networking offering the most hopeful prospects (see Hawken 2007). Communal empowerment carries an even deeper appeal as growing numbers of contemporary adults are losing faith in mainline governments also.

For the adult seekers today, an issue such as the divinity of Jesus carries little import. Jesus is seen as the primary disciple (catalyst) of the Companionship of Empowerment, whose God-like inspiration is embodied first and foremost in his humanity, the radiant face of God in our midst. It is this new empowering and liberating humanity that awakens hope and meaning in the hearts of contemporary adult seekers.

Adults find the parable stories of the Gospels deeply inspiring and engaging; they suggest to the imagination alternative ways of being and doing, and readers seek out strategies for empowerment in the name of liberation and enduring justice. The miracle narratives also challenge and inspire, not as evidence for the divinity of Jesus but as parable-type actions liberating people from systemic oppression and the internalized pain and suffering ensuing therefrom.

For contemporary adults, fidelity to the Companionship of Empowerment translates into new forms of engagement largely unknown in earlier Christian times. These new forms can be deeply disturbing to those who feel they have the primary responsibility for upholding Christian orthodoxy. The following are some of the emerging ideas engaging adults in this new understanding of their Christian faith:

1. We are people *with* the book, rather than people *of* the book! The Gospels are a resource with empowering potential, forever inviting us into deeper discernment of the meaning and challenge of the Word of God.
2. Christian discipleship is an invitation into a collaborative endeavor for co-creating a world characterized by empowering justice, liberation, and joy.
3. Christian faith is not so much about submission to a set of dogmatic truths, but it is rather an earth-based praxis focused on making the world a more God-like place.

4. The historical Jesus is viewed as the primordial disciple of the Companionship of Empowerment, offering a blueprint for discipleship that all Christians are challenged to embrace.

5. Christian mission requires collaboration with a range of agencies—religious and otherwise—to guarantee delivering programs and outcomes that will be experienced as empowering.

6. All pastoral undertakings must be valued in terms of empowering potential, rather than seeking to pacify people with vague promises of utopian hope.

7. People will need to be skilled to deliver a prophetic critique of all agencies and structures that collude with patriarchal power, for example the examination system extensively adopted in Western educational institutions.

8. The secular/political strategy of equal opportunities adopted by several contemporary Western governments should be viewed within the radical inclusiveness of the Companionship of Empowerment.

9. Implications for church practice—for example, the celebration of sacraments—will be explored in chapter 5.

Salvation Through the Cross

The Gospel emphasis on the death and resurrection of Jesus poses several challenges for adult faith today. "Why all the gory details?" they often ask. Why is the emphasis on suffering and martyrdom required for salvation? Adults suspect that the emphasis on suffering is an ecclesiastical ploy to cow people into submission and obedience (cf. Moss 2013). Keep reminding people of their unworthiness, and it is much easier to exert control over them.

Adult people of faith believe that the historical Jesus suffered to bring about the new Reign of God—the empowering companionship—but such suffering was endured in his life and ministry and not merely in his death. At the time, crucifixion was a death reserved for subversives; it tended to be a quick, brutal affair in which the prevailing powers sought to get rid of an empowering, subversive prophet. For reflective adults today, there is nothing salvific or holy about the brutal death of Jesus; rather they regard it as the prophetic price paid for a life radically and fully lived. The Resurrection of Jesus is viewed as a mystical-type endorsement for a life fully lived, and therefore should be linked with the life of Jesus and not with his death.

For adult faith seekers of our time, the notions of *salvation* and *redemption* are highly problematic. Enduring life in this world while we await the fullness of life in a heavenly hereafter denotes an escapist spirituality not congruent with the challenge of adult faith. The spirituality of escapism tends to be replaced with one of *engagement*. Increasingly, adults feel that we need to face our own human contribution to the mess we experience in the contemporary world; it is we who have created it, and it is up to us to resolve it. And Jesus offers us a model—primarily through his life— on how to engage more creatively and responsibly with the earth entrusted to our care.

Two interrelated issues require our attention. The first one is the notion of individual salvation in a life beyond made possible for us through the death and resurrection of Jesus. Traditionally, this has been the primary goal of Christian faith—and it still is for many Christians around the world. Transforming the present world in accordance with the vision of the Companionship of Empowerment (kingdom of God) feels like a gross distraction for many traditional Christians. Several years ago, the German theologian Jürgen Moltmann grappled with this dilemma and concludes:

> In the degree to which Christianity cut itself off from its Hebrew roots and acquired Hellenistic and Roman form, it lost its eschatological hope and surrendered its apocalyptic alternative to "this world" of violence and death. It merged into late antiquity's Gnostic religion of redemption. From Justin onwards, most Fathers revered Plato as a "Christian before Christ" and extolled his feelings for the divine transcendence and for the values of the spiritual world. God's eternity now took the place of God's future, heaven replaced the coming kingdom, the spirit that redeems the soul from the body supplanted the Spirit as "the well of life," the immortality of the soul displaced the resurrection of the body, and the yearning for another world became a substitute for changing this one. (Moltmann 1992, 89)

Contemporary adult Christians are more attuned to the "eschatological" calling of earthly and human transformation in accordance with the vision of the Companionship of Empowerment. This approach also seems more congruent with the Christian notion of *Incarnation*, celebrating and co-creating with the God who fully immerses Godself in the human and earthly project of making this world a wholesome place for all God's creatures.

In this dispensation there is no salvific rationale for exonerating suffering for its own sake. Like the historical Jesus, we embrace suffering in life (and not merely in death) in order to rid the world of all meaningless suffering. Martyrdom for its own sake has no place in "eschatological" adult Christianity. This is vividly portrayed by Brock and Parker (2008) in their review of the early Christian catacombs where—they claim—we find no images of a crucified Jesus, nor of a God in judgment, but instead a vast array of luxuriant images of nature with life in full bloom. This imagery they interpret as that of martyrs sacrificing their lives, not for the sake of salvation in a world beyond, but because they saw their suffering and death as a contribution to bringing about paradise on earth—depicted through the many scenic landscapes that decorate the Roman catacombs.

Paradise is a confusing concept, widely regarded as the ideal redemptive resolution in a life hereafter. Brock and Parker (2008) highlight the fact that this understanding of paradise belongs almost entirely to the second Christian millennium, when the doctrine of atonement heavily influenced the Christian theology of salvation and redemption. Throughout the first Christian millennium, paradise had a very different meaning, namely the transformation of our earthly reality into the new world order envisaged in the Christian notion of the Companionship of Empowerment.

Incarnational Humanity

For contemporary adults, Christianity exerts a strong appeal —and an even stronger challenge—to incarnate anew in our world the radical relational empowerment originally modeled by the historical Jesus in the project conventionally known as the Kingdom of God. As a mode of engagement (and not escape), the enterprise revolves around these central faith convictions:

1. The historical Jesus belongs to a significant moment in the 7,000,000-year evolutionary story of the human race, affirming, confirming, and celebrating all that humans had achieved throughout that trajectory, and serving as a bridge pointing humanity to its next major evolutionary breakthrough.

2. Consequently, the uniqueness of Jesus rests on a radical new way of being human, embodied within a social matrix known conventionally as the Kingdom of God (with the *Companionship of Empowerment* as one possible renaming in an attempt to honor the original Aramaic language of the historical Jesus).

3. This new articulation of embodied humanity transcends Aristotelian individuality and is grounded instead in relational wholeness. The historical Jesus is better understood as a relational "we" rather than an isolated "I"—the new Companionship serving as the relational web of his individual identity. The "Kingdom" is his extended persona.

4. For a growing body of contemporary adult faith seekers, the divinity of Jesus is of little or no importance. They feel they have more than enough to wrestle with in the radical new way of being human outlined above. And they suspect that divinity can be accessed and realized only through the humanity of Jesus.

5. Christian discipleship for contemporary adults is not about imitating the individual Jesus (or even praying to him). Rather it involves radical commitment to co-discipleship with Jesus in bringing to fuller realization on earth the new Companionship, initially launched by Jesus and now entrusted to the Christian people as Christ's body on earth.

6. Discipleship, therefore, is not about allegiance to a set of doctrines, or fidelity to church practices, but rather to the advancement of those *key values* embedded in the new Companionship: love, justice, empowerment, liberation, healing, and care for all entrusted to our care.

7. The notion of a Christian church is increasingly problematic for many adult faith seekers of our time. They react negatively to the overlay of patriarchal baggage and the power/control-structures which they detect as deeply alien to the Gospel vision. They fully support the social dimensions of faith and long for a church that is egalitarian, empowering, and committed to effective networking (more in chapter 5).

8. Those in the evolving adult generation also seek to integrate their Christian faith with the big questions facing humanity today: cosmic vision, wholesome earth ecology, economic justice, people-based politics, an end to violence and warfare, and transformation of all systems that engender poverty and oppression.

9. Bringing about heaven on earth is the goal that challenges and inspires the new generation of adult believers. Engaged commitment to earthly and human transformation is their understanding of Christian salvation. Life after death is an issue they trustingly leave to the universe and to the God who cares for all life.

10. In many of these matters, the evolving understanding of the Christian God is remarkably close to what indigenous peoples call the Great Spirit—the subject of our next chapter.

For Personal/Group Reflection

• How do you feel about being described as a Christian?

• How has your understanding of Christian faith changed over the years?

• What are your feelings about the description of the Kingdom of God as the Companionship of Empowerment?

• How do you perceive the Christian churches matching up to the challenges of the Christian Gospel?

Chapter Four

Faith in the Holy Spirit

The Spirit who has always been at work in us is in full control, drawing us into a future beyond all imagining.

— Benigno P. Beltran

Prayer is nothing but inhaling and exhaling the one breath of the Universe.

— Hildegard of Bingen

Regular churchgoers can readily predict the homily for Pentecost Sunday. It will be based on the first reading from Acts 2:1–11, describing the gathering of the reconstituted twelve apostles, with Mary, assembled in the upper room. Amid the ecstatic tongues of flame, they rediscover their faith in Jesus and go forth to proclaim the Good News with renewed zest and vigor.

The more observant worshipper may notice that the preacher has largely if not totally ignored the second part of that same reading, Acts 2:5–11, which describes a diverse group of listeners, many of whom have not been converted or proselytized. Nonetheless, these people are capable of hearing, understanding, and assimilating what the others are preaching. Those in this latter group are using all the skills popularly associated with the *discernment of spirits*, an accomplishment deemed to be impossible unless one is already imbued with the gifts of the Holy Spirit.

So, what is going on in this intriguing text? Despite the fact that, according to conventional Christian faith, the Holy Spirit is not conferred until Pentecost, it seems that the second group is already endowed with a fullness of the Spirit empowering them to discern deeply. Could it be that they enjoy the fullness of the Holy Spirit because according to Genesis 1:2, the Spirit already inhabits the whole creation from the beginning of time? Presumably every creature within that creation is also imbued with the Spirit's influence.

In which case, what is going on for the first group on that unique Pentecost day? Could it be that this is the group that was so shattered and disillusioned after the untimely death of Jesus that they needed a fresh infusion of the Spirit in order to resume the task of discipleship? In which case, we are witnessing the Spirit at work in a twofold articulation: (a) the reawakening of faith in the apostles empowering them to preach and teach, and (b) the spontaneous response of the Spirit in the diverse assembled group discerning the deep meaning of what they were hearing. I suspect it is *the second group*, rather than the first, that is expressing a deeper sense of the Spirit's empowerment.

The Spirit Who Blows Where It Will

Throughout Christian history, the Holy Spirit has not fared well. The third person of the Trinity effectively translates into the last of the sacred triad, incapable of exercising its influence until Father and Son are well established and have carried out their rescue strategy for flawed humanity. The patriarchal line of descent is unmistakable. This is a very different understanding from the notion of the Great Spirit upheld by indigenous people throughout the contemporary world. In the native wisdom, the Spirit comes first, and everything else, including divine activity, happens under the influence of the Great Spirit (more in O'Murchu 2012).

Throughout the twentieth century, we note several attempts by Christian theologians to rehabilitate the Holy Spirit into a more creative trinitarian dynamic. Interestingly, it was also throughout the twentieth century that we witnessed a huge Pentecostal revival, with Pentecostal churches today flourishing while other Christian churches struggle to survive. Not everybody is enamored of the excessive devotion, and occasionally bizarre behavior, of Pentecostals, but as a global movement, they embody a spiritual and cultural significance that deserves a much deeper discernment. They are a sign of our times, highlighting another dimension of adult faith appropriation in the contemporary world.

When we combine the Pentecostal revival with the renewed interest in the indigenous notion of the Great Spirit, we detect a spiritual awakening with particular appeal to adult sensibilities. The following features are particularly attractive:

- The Spirit denotes a sense of creativity and freedom transcending the patriarchal urge to dominate and control.
- The Spirit infuses the search for meaning throughout all religions and even beyond them.
- The Spirit is the primary energizer of creation, opening up several pregnant connections with modern science.
- The Spirit's creative energy evokes a theology of befriending rather than one of patriarchal domination.
- The feminine connection suggests a wide and empowering embrace.
- We glimpse a deep meaning in Pauline allusions to the Spirit, who empowers even Jesus (see Rom. 1:4; 8:11).
- The human invitation to become co-creators with Holy Wisdom begets a dynamic and engaging spirituality.

Enter the Transpersonal

Christian spirituality prioritizes the notion of a personal God, whereas theology describes Father, Son, and Holy Spirit as persons in their own right. For conventional Christians it is this personal relationship with the Holy One that confers faith and engenders deep meaning. Prayer and devotion are often expressed as if God and Jesus are persons just like we are, yet of transcendent nature. Christians quickly point out that the concept of the Great Spirit seems very impersonal compared to the Christian notion of Father or Jesus, who are perceived to be more intimately personal than the Great Spirit.

We are dealing with underlying assumptions—some metaphysical, others anthropological—which need to be reconsidered. The Aristotelian understanding of the human person looms large and heavily influences our understanding of the human even to the present day. For Aristotle a human person is defined by separation and isolation: true human personhood is separate from everything else in creation, must be unambiguously differentiated from all other (soulless) creatures, and must be rescued from the enmeshment in the natural world that—allegedly—characterized the primitive stages of our evolution as a human species.

The human person for Aristotle is totally unique and different from every other organism. Humans stand alone and apart from everything else and are deemed closer to God than any other creature. Moreover, humans are characterized by one outstanding quality: *the power of reasoning*, a superior gift that relegates and controls emotion and feeling, secondary characteristics that can distort the rational truth of life. The resilience of Aristotle's rationality can be seen in the late seventeenth century in John Locke's often quoted definition of a human person: "A thinking intelligent being that has reason and reflection, and can consider itself as itself, the same thinking thing, in different times and places."

Shaun Gallagher (1998) provides a fine overview and an extensive online bibliography on the subject of personalism. He concludes with these words:

> If there is consensus among personalists concerning the primacy and importance of the person, there is no dogma or unified doctrine that further constitutes a personalist ideology. Although the majority of personalists have been theists, there is no unified theology, or even a requirement that to be a personalist one must believe in God. There is no agreement about methods or definitions; indeed, even the definition of "personhood" remains an open question.

An open question in theory, but in fact quite a closed issue in the sense that the Aristotelian understanding enjoys an unquestioned hegemony in all forms of Western thought. Humans are characterized by a robust uniqueness that entitles them to be masters of God's creation. They represent the robust God, ruling from beyond the sky. That God has already been declared a male ruler and is, therefore, superior to the nebulous third person, often assumed to be feminine in its essential nature.

In popular Christian faith the Holy Spirit is often depicted as a dove and variously described as wind, air, fire, or energy. These are certainly not personal features, as we normatively understand personhood. Beyond the popular attributes is something much more subtle and profound, another understanding of personhood largely unknown to our time. It is another way of understanding the essence of humanity grounded in the sum of relationships that characterizes everything in the web of life. Relational human identity is often encapsulated in this phrase: *I am at all times the sum of my relationships and that's what constitutes my identity.* The Holy Spirit belongs to this mode of personhood, and not to the Aristotelian construct described above.

Biologically, in the case of each of us, relational personhood is mediated by parents, who facilitate one's entry into life: I come into the world through a relationship, and every stage of my growth and development is made possible through the interactive, relational dynamics of life. Relationship is the divine blueprint for all life-forms, the human included, a dimension of trinitarian theology highlighted by many scholars in the closing decades of the twentieth century (Taylor 1972; LaCugna 1991; Fox 2001; Johnson 2007).

Karen Armstrong (1993, 209–10) alerts Christians to this dangerous tendency to idolize Jesus and project on to him our needs, fears, and desires, depicting Jesus as one who loves what we love and hates what we hate. Such personalized faith, she suggests, is at best a stage in religious development rather than a mature adult appropriation of faith. A more mature articulation, embracing the relational understanding of personhood, is evidenced in mysticism and can be detected in several indigenous spiritualities, often dismissed as primitive by the advocates of formal religion.

The Spirit in Creation

Adult faith seekers are drawn today to the Spirit of God alive in creation. This is the transpersonal God, who embraces all that is personal while transcending it. This is not an impersonal cosmic force, a judgment rashly made by several contemporary fundamentalists and an allegation often made against our ancient ancestors and their animistic love for the natural world.

Today we experience a theological retrieval of the central role of the Holy Spirit in which animistic concepts can once more be honored. Theologians such as Mark Wallace (2005) seek to redeem the rich cosmic and spiritual meaning of metaphors like vivifying breath, healing wind, living water, and purifying fire. As we deepen our sense of the sacred at work in creation, these become liberating phrases to understand and comprehend the magnificence of God creatively animating, sustaining, and empowering life at every level.

The ensuing sense of faith moves from being merely a personal requirement to guarantee my personal salvation in a life beyond, to that of a communitarian endeavor engaging the sacred in the entire web of life, cosmic, planetary, social, and personal alike. And this earth-centered understanding of the Spirit is often the starting point at which contemporary adults begin to reconsider their inherited understanding of God. The anthropocentric (personal) grounding begins to feel narrow, congested, and humanly inflated; the adult seeker desires a more expansive understanding.

This expanded horizon is captured in these inspiring words of the late priest and geologist, Thomas Berry:

> As all creativity involves being seized by an archetypal reality in the unconscious depths of the universe, as creative religious personalities were seized by revelatory experiences of the divine whereby

they created the religious cultures of the past, so now we are being seized by a new revelatory experience that is coming to us in the new origin story and its fulfilment in this latest communion phase of the universe. It is the supreme challenge of our period to bring this new origin story into its fuller articulation. With this story as an orienting context, our way into the future is possible. (Berry 2006, 74)

Encountering the Spirit in the evolving process of creation itself is an experience that resonates deeply with adult faith seekers of this time. Mark Hathaway and Leonardo Boff captivate something of this contemporary mystical experience when they write:

The Spirit permeates all as an entanglement of the universe with itself; as an awakening of consciousness, desire, and enthusiasm; as a cry of liberation, and, as a force of communication and communion. This vision provides us with a cosmic-ecological mysticism. . . . We form a whole with and in the Spirit. To allow oneself to be imbued and filled by these processes is to live according to the Spirit in a natural and conscious manner. (Hathaway and Boff 2009, 329)

Quantum physics can contribute richly to this expansive role of the Spirit, and the American Sister Miriam Therese Winter (2009) has attempted a quantum-based pneumatology that will stretch the mind and soul of the most adventurous spiritual seeker. She re-visions the seven gifts of the Holy Spirit in terms of the wisdom of quantum physics. Instead of the human-centered list (wisdom, understanding, counsel, fortitude, knowledge, piety, and fear of the Lord), she proposes that we reimagine the gifts of the Spirit as those of *relativity, uncertainty, probability, complementarity, non-locality, synchronicity, and change.*

To appreciate the depth of this insight, the reader will need to transcend the anthropocentric bias for personalism. The new list feels very impersonal, until we begin to discern that all these words—from the quantum perspective—describe the essential relatedness, openness, surprise, expansiveness, and dynamism that causes everything in creation to grow and flourish. Without this hypercreative elegance, humans would not even exist, never mind thrive.

The dynamism of creation itself is the home of the Great Spirit, who unceasingly enlivens and draws forth order from chaos and emptiness. This is the life-force that classical science can never describe; it is the quantum-entangled terminology that reflects more accurately how the Spirit operates. Even for seeking adults, these are novel ideas, but ones that certainly inspire and empower.

Holy Spirit: Source of Archetypal Creativity

Here is another parable to engage the adult imagination in the twenty-first century:

> An African wildlife expert, Lawrence Anthony, created two new game reserves in his native South Africa seeking to involve remote African tribes in conservation on their own traditional land, an

activity he considered essential to the future well-being of conservation in Africa. Anthony is best known for the rehabilitation of traumatized African elephants. He had developed a unique relationship with a wild herd of elephant on the Thula Thula Reserve in Zululand. Anthony's second book, *The Elephant Whisperer*, tells the story of his working relationship with the rogue elephants.

On March 2, 2012, Anthony died of a heart attack at his home in South Africa's KwaZulu. Over the next 48 hours, elephants, who were grazing miles away in different parts of the park, travelled over 12 hours to reach his house. They hadn't visited the compound where Anthony lived for a year and a half. There are two elephant herds at Thula Thula. According to Anthony's son, Dylan, both arrived at the family home shortly after Anthony's death. The first herd arrived on Sunday and the second herd, a day later. They all hung around for about two days before making their way back into the bush.

They came to grieve the loss of a cherished friend and pay their respects to one who had transformed their future through his dedicated care.

How did the elephants know that Anthony had died? Why did different herds, who rarely mingle, synchronize their movement toward the same venue? Why did the elephants make the journey? And why did they all depart around the same time?

Experts in animal behavior consider *instinct* to be the basis of everything that animals do. Occasional exceptions

are put down to intuition or chance, but it is rare and
tends not to be repeated. I suggest that something deeper
is at work in the elephants that came to mourn the loss of
Lawrence Anthony. *Archetype* rather than *instinct* may be
the force at work, a creative energy in which things of the
Spirit grow and flourish.

What Is an Archetype?

The concept of archetypes is popularly associated with Jungian psychology, although the notion is also familiar to an-
thropologists studying the complexities of human behavior.
Carl Jung, in his *Answer to Job*, has described archetypes as
"transcendentally conditioned dynamisms, formative principles of instinctual power." According to this definition, an
internal psychic force, defying rational explanation, is what
we are dealing with. Its dynamism transforms our instinctual drives directing creative energy to serve more sublime
outcomes. Ultimately, the archetypes forge unity amid the
divergent forces of our psychological evolutionary growth.

The following examples from daily life highlight the
complementary nature of instinct and archetype.

Behavior	Instinct	Archetype
Sex	Pleasure, gratification	Capacity to bond intimately
Hunger	Survival, gratification	Nourishment for growth
Jealousy	To be as good as; inferiority	Yearning for completeness
Anger	Defense against threat	Justice and fair play
Power	Domination and control	Empowerment via mutuality

Every emotion is imbued with value and not merely driven by instinctual urge. All behavior can be viewed as a yearning for a greater wholeness, the ultimate goal of all spiritual (Spirit-filled) endeavor. Applying the archetypal to human behavior is quite a challenge for our patriarchal cultures preoccupied with exerting control, and—often inadvertently—evoking certain moral demands assuming the human condition to be essentially fickle, rebellious, and sinful. The archetypal perspective makes a foundational claim for the essential goodness of human desire, the ultimate, deeply subconscious pursuit of value, meaning, and purpose.

In such a culture it is virtually inconceivable that animals might also be endowed with archetypal intent. Researchers such as Jane Goodall, Frans de Waal, and a host of others highlight a range of alternative examples that require a much more nuanced assessment of animal behavior. We assume that the behavior of the elephants, engaging with Lawrence Anthony's death, is a rare exception. Perhaps it is not! Might it serve as an invitation to probe more deeply into what underpins and motivates behavior, human and nonhuman alike—all informed by the wisdom of the Great Spirit!

The Archetypal Cosmos

For many years now, the Jungian scholar James Hillman has been alerting us to the integral and extensive power of archetypal energy, not merely in humans, but at several levels of human and global culture. Insights of modern physics on the dynamic nature of energy reinforce Hillman's convictions. More recent scholarship pushes the archetypal horizon even further—to limits which the human mind can scarcely fathom.

In 2006, the cultural historian Richard Tarnas published a landmark book, *Cosmos and Psyche,* purporting that all archetypal energy is mediated through cosmic forces involving large-space context of planets and galaxies. The stars and planets do not merely affect our lives, our perceptions, emotions, and actions, but influence our likely patterns of behavior. Insights long held by astrologers and other esoteric visionaries are elevated as material for more serious scientific research.

Keiron Le Grice, of the San Francisco Institute of Integral Studies, provides access to the complex insights of Richard Tarnas. In his book *The Archetypal Cosmos,* Le Grice writes:

> Understood from a systems perspective, we might say that astrology enables us to understand how the self-organizing dynamics at work in the solar system are affecting human experience at any given time. The pattern of cyclic alignments of the planets is not just a physical pattern made up of lumps of rock, ice, and gas, orbiting the sun in meaningless mechanical motion; it is actually the external structural form of a meaningful underlying pattern of self-organization that shapes not only the visible planetary order of the solar system, but also the deeper dynamics of human experience. (Le Grice 2010, 112)

Combined with the wisdom of the New Cosmology and insights from the New Physics, Le Grice suggests that the archetypal realm belongs first and foremost to the cosmic and planetary domains, a pattern of deep meaning inscribed into the universe itself. Where does the universe inherit such wisdom from? Wisely, neither Le Grice nor Tarnas postulate God (as traditionally understood) as the source of this dynamic pattern. In conjunction with Jung and Hillman, Le Grice and Tarnas detect spiritual significance in their controversial insights but steer clear of formal religion in seeking an ultimate explanation.

Had Le Grice and Tarnas adopted the notion of the Great Spirit, as espoused by indigenous and tribal peoples throughout the contemporary world, they would have had a much more solid basis for what might well be described as *an archetypal spirituality*. Without a spiritual dimension to such considerations, we lack a crucial element in the explanatory process. Carl Jung himself was keenly aware of this foundational element which he attributed to the creative power of the divinity itself.

The Archetypal Adult?

Why these complex and controversial ideas in a book on adult faith development? It strikes me that a great deal of archetypal awakening is happening in the contemporary world, due to a range of evolutionary forces that characterize our time; this awakening is comprehensively described by David Abram (2010), Ilia Delio (2013), and Carter Phipps (2012). Those described as "adult" in the present book are the people most likely to feel the impact of such awakening. My hope is that this brief overview will alert adults to the deeper awakening they may be experiencing, and offer some resources for further exploration.

The dilemma confronting many of the adult people I write about is captured by Keiron Le Grice when he writes:

> The dominant mode of thinking today has become almost exclusively discursive. It is now factual, not symbolic, more literal than metaphorical, and predominantly rational rather than intuitive. Indeed, such is the one-sided dominance of analytical thought that the modern mind is subject to what Jung called a "cramp of consciousness," a neurotic condition in which, it is now widely recognized, we have grown dangerously out of alignment with the natural order of things, and with the unconscious foundations of our psychological experience. (Le Grice 2010, 124)

People all over the contemporary world are waking up to a larger sense of reality in the face of which our major institutions (politics, economics, social policy, education, and religion) become more defensive and retrogressive. It feels to me as if the adults are moving in one direction while our institutions veer the opposite way. And the gap is widening, leaving little hope for dialogue or a meaningful discernment on what is actually going on in our contemporary complex world.

Whereas our institutions seem to be reacting from the level of instinct, more adult people feel a call to respond to the inspiration of the archetypal. The wisdom from the ground up is outpacing what is coming from the top down. Major institutions are becoming more defensive and reactionary. They feel threatened by the evolving world of maturing adults, inspired by an archetypal awakening, which the dominant culture can nether appreciate nor embrace.

Worshipping in Spirit and in Truth

Indigenous peoples, either ancient or modern, do not worship the Great Spirit. Instead they strive to live in harmony with the Spirit's endeavors and respond to the Spirit's urgings—or the Spirit's archetypal awakenings. They participate in rituals, ceremonies marking seasons or life passages, and celebrations of communal or personal significance. In these rituals they may invoke the Great Spirit—for a good harvest, for healing, for reconciliation, or for a particular blessing—but such invocation is not addressed to a supernatural being beyond this world but to an empowering life-force perceived to be innate in creation itself. And the invocation is not that of powerless passive humans, addressing an all-powerful "divine" force. Rather it is closer to an evocation of an empowering potential that belongs as much to the ones invoking it as it does to the life-force invoked.

In religious or spiritual terms, we are entering a mystical space, as long as we remember that we are dealing with a very earthy mysticism, and not one focused on a transcendent being (or state) beyond this world. Nor must any semblance of dualism be entertained: the holy is both within and without; there is no room for a sacred-secular divide.

In indigenous cultures, everybody participates in ritual making, with elders playing leading roles. Properly understood, good ritual transcends the kind of codependent behavior that often begets formal religions. In indigenous rituals, people do not throw themselves at the mercy of God, beseeching an all-powerful deity to rescue or redeem them from perdition. Such worship is largely unknown in the bedrock traditions of first nations peoples around the world. (Under the influence of Christianity or Islam, such features

have crept in, and are particularly noticeable in tribal rituals
of African and Latino peoples.)

Today, we experience a renewed interest in first-nations
spirituality and the sacred within indigenous and tribal cultures. This is usually publicized in ecologically informed
concerns, whether related to current issues such as global
warming or the reclaiming of lands from which indigenous
peoples have been ousted. Subliminally, a great deal more is
going on here. I wish to suggest that the appeal has a deeply
personal and cultural significance, providing openings for
the kind of adult spirituality being explored in this book.

Belief in the Great Spirit arises from a culture of participation and mutual engagement. The lure of the Spirit in
the living earth itself both invites and prompts people into
creative engagement. From this engagement arise the crucial values that sustain and empower indigenous peoples.
Holy mystery dwells in the living web of life, in which every
thing has an interdependent place, and every creature—humans and otherwise—manifests the creative potential of
the Great Spirit. The entire system is poised for the evolution of an adult kind of faith.

Central to the maturation of faith is an understanding of God (or Holy mystery) that is particularly baffling
for monotheistic religions and for Christianity specifi-
cally. There is no trace of an omnipotent, omniscient deity. There is no "personal" God with whom humans can
have a "personal" relationship. And there is no need for
religious institutions or ecclesiastical enclaves. Yet for indigenous peoples, sacredness is very real, and the Great
Spirit has a deeply personal significance for such peoples.
And there are religious structures (albeit quite flexible

and adaptable to various contexts)—as well as unambiguous moral and spiritual values.

In these long-neglected spiritual traditions, we find articulations of faith that appeal deeply to adult spiritual sensibilities of the present time. They provide cultural models that can be adopted by adults today and used to inspire and evolve ways of engaging with Holy Mystery that feel more congruent and empowering than traditional ways. Central to this inherited wisdom is the notion of the Great Spirit, the significance of which I have explored in detail in a previous work (O'Murchu 2012).

How the notion of the Great Spirit might inform the Christian notion of the Holy Spirit is an exploration theologians have not even yet embraced. One informative starting point would be to examine closely the unfolding spiritual dreams and aspirations of modern adult faith seekers. The lure of the Spirit is central to adult maturation and manifests particularly in the following features, attested to in many parts of the contemporary world:

1. Adults tend to be more attracted to the God within rather than to the external landmarks by which our world tends to judge religious allegiance. Hence the popularity of meditation, interiority, and stillness for many adult spiritual seekers today.

2. Adults intuit the spirit of God to be alive in a distinctive way in the living creation itself. New scientific insight on the meaning of energy and field influence helps adults understand this internalized spirit-force.

3. That sense of inner living spirit evokes for adults a quality of unity that transcends all human divisions; it can bring healing to our damaged earth, peace beyond global violence, and a force for reconciliation beyond the voracious competitiveness that characterizes our world today.

4. Adult creativity comes more alive in ritual participation focused on the Great Spirit and its central role in the in-spirited creation than in traditional rituals. Consequently, how sacraments are celebrated in conventional churches often leaves contemporary adults with a sense of "something missing." They experience something more in creative rituals.

5. An adult faith with a strong focus on spirit evokes great hope to confront and outgrow the pessimism and despair of our time, as the Spirit forever lures people forth into a deeper commitment to work for justice, equality, and truth in our world.

6. Perhaps most challenging—and inspiring—of all is the new sense of God and divine meaning that is evoked in this fresh appreciation of a Spirit-infused creation—the broad strokes of which are outlined in chapter 2.

For Personal/Group Reflection

- Has your understanding of the Holy Spirit changed over the years?
- In the practice of your faith what practical difference does belief in the Holy Spirit make?

- What are your feelings about the indigenous notion of the Great Spirit, as the primary understanding of God or universal mystery?
- What is your personal experience of the Spirit at work in creation?
- Pentecostal movements flourish today. Why do you think that is so?

Chapter Five

Faith in the Church

This is the issue: either the Church sees and recognizes the essential differences of other cultures for which she should become a world Church, and with Pauline boldness draws the necessary consequences from this recognition, or she remains a Western Church and so in the final analysis betrays the meaning of Vatican II.

— Karl Rahner

For the contemporary adult faith seeker, it is the church rather than religious belief that creates several serious dilemmas. The disconnect between church reality and the challenges of a vibrant faith grow wider by the day. And it is not merely all the baggage of an outdated institution; foundationally, it is a deep suspicion that this way of structuring religious belief may not even be of God. Is the church yet another anthropocentric construct born out of, and sustained by, patriarchal power-mongering?

Such unease arises from a wide disillusionment that characterizes our time. Reflective adults today are wary of all dominant institutions. Trust in political, economic, and social systems has significantly declined in recent times. This has resulted from our information-saturated culture where people are far more aware of what is going on behind the scenes and can critically discern the corruption and exploitation sustaining many contemporary institutions. The resentment is all the more intractable because there are no obvious channels through which the perceived malaise can be addressed or rectified. People can vote to change a government but can do very little to activate change during the duration of an administration's existence.

Those who can penetrate the systems and expose wrong-doings, for example, Julian Assange's WikiLeaks, are fiercely criticized and purported to be a threat to public security. In truth, they provide a prophetic clarion call for truth and transparency, and serve an important cultural affirmation for all seeking a more adult way of behaving in the contemporary world.

Church at Its Origins

Church is very much a Christian idea, although similar social constructs do exist in most major world religions. As a Christian concept, it belongs to Saint Paul rather than to Jesus. In Paul's time, the *ecclesia* was a political unit, similar to the town or city council, and it consisted only of men. Paul borrowed this political concept and used it to describe the gatherings of early Christians for fellowship, prayer, and charitable outreach.

The Pauline ecclesial groups—what today might be called house-churches—were small enough to be intimate, and they were flexible, minimally structured, and socially oriented to justice and inclusion. Paul visited many such groups in Asia Minor, Greece, and as far as Rome, affirming, advising, and encouraging their efforts to embrace the vision of Jesus. Of particular significance was the inclusive composition of these gatherings; contrary to their political counterparts, they consisted of both men and women (although I acknowledge that the women had to assume more passive roles than the men). Paul strove to lay ecclesiastical foundations that were inclusive, flexible, empowering, and devoid of the patriarchal overlay that would later infiltrate Christianity. (For a fine overview, see Page 2012.)

This infiltration got the strongest validation from Constantine's imperial vision. He is the one who rechristened Jesus as the *Pantocrator* (ruler of the whole universe) and set in place a kinglike imperial structure in the church that continues to our own time, providing the foundational understanding of bishops and other hierarchical leaders in all the Christian denominations.

This collusion with secular imperial power alienates modern adult believers. Many who have studied spirituality or theology know the historical background, as well as the patriarchal ideology of clinging rigidly to all that has been sanctioned from the past. This cult of continuity is postulated as if it were a divine mandate—anything solemnly declared in church teaching can never be abrogated—but many adults today regard such allegiance to the past as rigid, unreflective fidelity to patriarchal power.

This collusion with top-down structures and values also reinforces the unease around church allegiance. "How can an institution, so closely wedded to patriarchal domination, claim fidelity to the empowering justice of the Christian Gospel" the adult seeker asks. Where is the congruence between the values of the New Reign promulgated by Jesus and the collusion with man-made imperialism? This mismatch irks and alienates many adults exploring their faith commitment today.

Guardian of Truth

The inherited patriarchal dominance relates not merely to structures; much more significantly, it seeks to control both the content and flow of knowledge and information. Now that we live in a world of mass information, with adult people much more critically aware, the church's traditional guardianship of knowledge is under severe strain. The church still strives to control the knowledge content by invoking concepts such as *revelation* and *inspiration* of Scripture, and the timeworn cliché of the church's teaching authority. Attempts to silence theologians and creative thinkers merely alienate people—and once again, it is predominantly reflective lay adults who shift their allegiance in terms of church commitment.

The following are among the problematic elements for questioning adults today:

- The conventional Christian understanding of *revelation* is far too narrow and anthropocen-

tric. God's revelation comes to us first and foremost through the surrounding creation. It is an
evolving, expanding wisdom, which should not
be confined to any one religion or denominational system.

• The *inspiration of Scripture* is deemed to be a
highly spurious claim. Historically the Canon
of Scripture was compiled during the third and
fourth centuries, by a group of European, elite
males. Females had no say whatever in the matter, nor was there any attempt to include the
wisdom of the other creatures inhabiting God's
creation. By definition, this understanding of inspiration is elitist, sexist, exclusively European,
imperialistic, and anthropocentric. Little wonder
that contemporary adults are so dismissive of the
notion of canonical inspiration.

• The anthropocentric notions of revelation
and canonical inspiration also feed into a
sense of suspicion—shared by both reflective
adults and a growing body of Scripture scholars—that other noncanonical Scriptures may
contain valuable information and wisdom re-
garding the foundations and origins of Christian faith. Nowadays, the Gospel of Thomas
is often cited alongside the four canonical
Gospels, and the Gospel of Mary has been extensively studied amid a growing interest in
the role of Mary Magdalene in the life and
ministry of Jesus.

- Increasing numbers of lay people suspect there is more to Gospel wisdom than what the text literally states. *Literal interpretation* evokes a lot of questions for modern adults. The need to interpret Scripture and to honor insights not approved by formal churches is much more widely accepted.

- The imperial tenor of the Gospels—what contemporary scholars describe as *the postcolonial overlay*—is another area of adult suspicion. All the rhetoric about the kingship of God and Jesus seems to be much more about the imperial culture of the day than about divine, revealed truth. And the growing conviction (among scholars) that Jesus totally rejected the culture of violent imperialism carries a deep appeal for reflective adults in our time.

- A similar suspicion prevails around the incorporation of *Greek metaphysics* into early church thinking, especially in the Christological doctrines of Nicaea and Chalcedon. For instance, the individualized understanding of personhood, borrowed from Greek philosophy, is perceived today to be quite alien to the relational understanding espoused by the historical Jesus (more in O'Murchu 2011, 42–55).

- A growing body of adults warms to the more critical stance of the Jesus Seminar in the United States, which sought to establish what is likely to be genuinely historical and what has been added either by journalistic standards of the

time or because of other cultural and literary influences. And such critical analysis does not undermine religious allegiance for evolving adults
today; it actually enriches and deepens their faith
in Jesus.

Because adults of our time have become more intellectually aware than in the past, they raise more penetrating
questions and expect answers that are more honest and
transparent. Today, they feel that more often they have
to pursue these answers outside, rather than within, the
church; sometimes this results in people being driven away
from the church (in its formal sense).

The frustration in accessing adult wisdom within the
church can be seen as a deficiency in the dominant structures adopted by the church today. Despite all the rhetoric
of Vatican II, the Catholic Church remains heavily clericalized, with a huge proportion of clergy either unaware of, or
ambivalent about, the serious questioning of contemporary
adults.

Therefore, the pursuit of adult dialogue will need to go
hand in hand with the development of participative, collaborative structures. Initially, these may need to happen more
outside the formal institution rather than within. When
adults themselves become more self-confident at co-creating
forums for dialogue and adult discernment, then there may
be a greater possibility to convince the formal church of the
need for a different and more empowering set of structures
amenable not merely to questioning adults but indeed to
all those seeking a more participative church for the future.
Historically, we do have some generative models, with quite

a checkered history in a church occasionally leaning toward greater inclusivity, but consistently withdrawing when it feels that its monopoly of power is threatened.

Basic Ecclesial Communities

The church never totally lost its allegiance to the foundational sense of empowering local community. Interpersonal interaction and support have been the hallmarks of living faith for much of the Christian era, albeit frequently in spite of the formal church rather than with its approval. The potential of such witness flowered once again in the closing decades of the twentieth century with the rise of Basic Ecclesial Communities (BECs) in many parts of the Christian world. One got the impression that this was a widespread development when in fact it was quite localized. For instance, in the Catholic Church of Brazil—throughout the 1980s—about 10 percent of Catholics participated in BECs, suggesting that 90 percent remained faithful to more conventional church practice. Yet, the originality and creativity represented by that 10 percent proved to be so authentic and empowering that it sent inspiring vibrations throughout the entire Christian world.

This is the type of church the modern adult seeker desires, a forum that provides an outlet for the following features of participation:

- small enough for people to know each other in a personal and intimate way
- conducive to storytelling as a medium to explore the journey of faith

- skilled in dialogue so as to experience the empowering potential of the Scriptures
- creative enough to explore a range of life-enhancing rituals (liturgies)
- adopting ethical values, not merely confined to private personal behavior
- a space to know the warmth and reassurance of God's love through the quality and depth of human interaction
- participative learning on how to facilitate pastoral leadership, within and beyond the community itself
- practical channels for outreach to the poor and marginalized
- practical networking with the wider human family to support the work of ecojustice around the world
- opportunities to explore faith in other cultural contexts, e.g., mysticism, multifaith dialogue, and meditation

Participation is the central feature of this endeavor, reechoing the words of John's Gospel: "I do not call you servants anymore, but friends." And that friendship empowers and liberates service of God through serving other people, and engaging the larger creation in an organic and ecologically sustainable way. It leads to that prophetic dialogue highlighted by Stephen Bevans and Robert Schroeder (2011) as the central value of Christian mission today.

Networking the Networks

Time is rapidly catching up to all major institutions in the contemporary world, as we detect growing evidence of fragmentation, intransigence, and irrelevance. The struggle of Barack Obama to deliver and implement a national health service in the United States is a timely example, reminding us of the enormous obstacles that major institutions create to inhibit or undermine that which will empower people, particularly the poor and socially disenfranchised. Paradoxically, religious groups, including the Catholic hierarchy, often reinforced the opposition to Obama's health bill, on ethical principles that failed to embrace larger moral issues. This is often what alienates reflective adults, making people, both young and old, cynical about and dismissive of church teaching in general.

In the opening decade of the twenty-first century we evidenced in both the United States and Europe a great deal of economic turmoil with parliamentarians and economists scrambling to shore up a crumbling capitalistic system. Both political and economic institutions betrayed a distinctive lack of creative imagination—of the type exemplified by the alternative economic visionary, Charles Eisenstein (2011). In Gospel terms it very much felt like pouring new wine into old wineskins, holding on desperately to what worked in the past, reinforcing the power of those already in control, and making life precarious and problematic for the increasing numbers of people consigned to struggle and to an uncertain future.

Crises of this nature are likely to dominate life throughout much of the twenty-first century, and people

who have acquired an adult capacity for critical thinking—particularly wise elders—all too easily detect the institutional flaws. No longer will such adults opt to change
things from within, where they know they will meet huge
resistance. More intuitively and subversively, they will
look out for creative alternatives. To the fore is the power
of *networking*.

Paul Hawken (2007) provides one of the more acces-
sible overviews of how networking functions in the modern
world. As we enter the twenty-first century, two distinctive
developments command our attention. First, we are confronted with systemic problems of a global nature (global
warming, poverty, violence, etc.), which can no longer be
resolved by individual governments acting in isolation, and
in several cases, the problems seem resistant to formal governments acting collaboratively (e.g., the war on terror).
Second, we see a worldwide movement of small groups de-
termined to heal the wounds of the earth with the force
of passion, dedication, and indigenous wisdom. Across the
planet, groups ranging from ad hoc neighborhood associations to well-funded international organizations are confronting issues like the destruction of the environment, the
abuses of free market capitalism, social justice, and the loss
of indigenous cultures.

These two parallel movements converge in a strangely
unexpected way. The latter culture of networking has
become the conscience that pushes formal governments
into urgent action. And this has been the case throughout
the closing decades of the twentieth century—right up to
the present time. Issues like the hole in the ozone layer,

deforestation, biodiversity, threatened species, and global warming became issues of governmental concern—nationally and internationally—only when the alarming evidence provided by networks such as Greenpeace, Friends of the Earth, Worldwatch, and several local ecology groups could no longer be ignored. Sadly, the media tend to highlight governmental response to these crises but rarely give credit to those who forced governments into facing the harsh truth in the first place.

Millions of networks exist around our world, many activating and enhancing empowerment in ways major institutions are unable to deliver. And yet, the networking is not making a strong or overt impact. It appears that the next crucial evolutionary stage will be that of the *networking of the networks*. Then the counterrevolution is likely to become much more visible—and culturally more credible. That achievement is not likely to transpire without a more coherent global spirituality (see Phipps 2012), a conviction held by several adult faith seekers, although not widely acknowledged.

Involvement in networking can at times be tedious, chaotic, and frustrating. And when the network works, the sense of satisfaction can be exhilarating. In either case, information is the primary stuff being negotiated. This often involves a steep learning curve, and in this new evolutionary landscape we never cease learning. Networking flourishes on a philosophy of life that is considerably different from mainstream culture, where some provide the knowledge and skill while most remain passive observers. In good networking, distinctions between elite and rank-and-file break down. Mutuality, participation, and collaboration constitute the modus operandi. And the shift in awareness—the new consciousness—is crucial. This is the dream—and the hope—which is central to adult faith in our time.

Although many governments collaborate with networks—covertly for the greater part—and in many parts of the world local governance tends to follow the networking philosophy of fluidity, flexibility, and maximum participation, the power of networking is subverted for the greater part. It has little or no place in formal educational programs other than in multimedia studies. And millions of people, still deluded by the lure of glamour and power, are unaware of this major cultural transition. With the increasing awareness of the challenge to more authentic adulthood, the trend toward networking is likely to hold out enormous hope, with prospects of a more empowering and grace-filled future.

A New Ecclesial Horizon

Every Christian church today strives to be collaborative, inclusive, and empowering—unknowingly endorsing the networking vision. And yet the churches are failing to attract or engage substantial numbers of people. Moreover, adult faith seekers are not impressed by such ecclesial endeavors. Perhaps it feels like too little too late. Or is it more of an adult critical perception that genuinely novel strategies are not possible within the old framework? Something more original and inspiring is needed. And certainly a church modeled more on networking principles looks like a more viable and empowering possibility.

Many of the adults I write about in this book do retain varying degrees of attachment with formal churches.

Rarely, however, are they satisfied with what they receive or with the levels at which their churches respond to the pressing issues of our time. And although many of those same adults retain a degree of affiliation with a local church, they also look elsewhere—to conferences, workshops, networking groups, and so on—for the fulfillment of their spiritual and theological needs. In the future, the churches may not be able to hold on to these questing and questioning adults, as they are likely to become more critical in their perceptions, more demanding in terms of mutual engagement, and more subversive in pursuit of a church that can play a more prophetic role in the evolving world of our time.

In ecclesial terms, these will probably be the crucial issues that will engage future adult faith seekers:

- The UN strategy of *think globally and act locally* characterizes the ecclesiology being sought and pursued by contemporary people of adult faith.
- The strategy more likely to produce such an outcome is that of networking, with the model of the Basic Ecclesial Community (BEC) as the closest approximation in current church practice.
- The networking philosophy appeals mainly because it is perceived to be empowering in a way that conventional church practice fails to realize.
- Networking strongly emphasizes the mobilization of diverse gifts, particularly from the base upward, and it seems to achieve this goal far more effectively than conventional church practice.

- The strong collaborative tenor of networking appeals to adults as a way of challenging and reframing the dysfunctional authoritarian styles of leadership often adopted in the churches.
- Theologically, the networking vision seems to provide an authentic process for implementing on our earth the Gospel vision of the Kingdom of God (Companionship of Empowerment).
- The spirituality of networking seeks to transcend the dualistic split between the sacred and the secular, adopting instead a holistic vision with strong appeal to adult faith in our time.
- For today's adult lay missionary, networking connotes dialogue and collaboration with diverse religious and cultural traditions, very different from the traditional proselytizing approach, characteristic of earlier times.

Gathered for Worship

It is in the area of worship, more than any other, that adult Christians often feel estranged and alienated, and hindered by a range of stipulations prohibiting liturgical changes they deeply desire. Sometimes the problem rests with a particular pastor, or diocesan structure, seeking to retain control and monopoly of all sacramental practice. Other times, it is the ritualistic rigidity of ecclesiastical norms and guidelines. More recently, in the Catholic context, it is the estrangement caused by a style of language (literal imitation of the Latin) that fails to captivate people's real lived experience and sometimes sounds so convoluted that its actual meaning is not even apparent.

In its original meaning the word *liturgy* is derived from the Greek *leitourgia*, denoting free labor from wealthy citizens to augment the growth of the city-state (*polis*). It has strong associations with work through generous service. It is valuable to recall this root meaning to ensure that both Christian service—and worship—are always grounded in the domestic issues of daily life. This is what the enterprise of the new Companionship is all about; both spirituality and worship need to serve this undertaking.

In *Adult Faith* (171–74), I highlight the three stages humanity has come through in our collective internalization of the need for meaningful worship. First is the capacity for ritual making, which humans have been exercising for over seventy thousand years, long before the evolution of formal churches and their various sacramental systems. The capacity for ritual making is a God-given endowment that intuitively every adult knows and cherishes. It is an innate, God-given potential.

In time, ritual making evolved into more widely identifiable structures known as rites of passage, still observable among indigenous peoples today. These are special ceremonies marking significant life stages, seasonal transformations, or cultural celebrations around food and reconciliation. Such celebrations were adopted and endured over time and across cultures precisely because they were experienced as empowering and liberating for those involved. Clearly, these are precursors to the Christian notion of sacrament, although few Christian theologians acknowledge this ancient and enduring source.

Linking past with present time, it may be worth recalling that indigenous peoples around the world do not worship the Great Spirit; instead, they seek to *co-create* with it. Perhaps this is where we need to start in engaging with the adult desire of our time for more flexibility and creativity in ritual making and worship. It is the basis of the Pauline understanding of all Christian prayer: it is not we who pray, but the Spirit of God who prays within us (see Rom. 8:26). Christian devotion, prayer, and worship are more about creating a disposition of openness to the living Spirit who imbues what the heart desires in every realm of our daily lives.

Not surprisingly, therefore, we experience in the modern world a desire for stillness and interiority, which often leads to the adoption of one or other meditation practice. Millions learned to meditate throughout the latter half of the twentieth century, and these were predominantly adults, seeking to internalize and deepen their connection with Holy Mystery.

Correspondingly, these are some of the same people who criticize public worship for being excessively verbose, legalistic, and clericalized. However, we also need to note the huge popularity of Pentecostal worship, with a distinctive focus on song, dance, body movement, and joyful celebration. Adult worship in the future will be challenged to integrate these two apparently diverse elements, accommodating the stillness of solitude alongside the use of exuberant embodied ritual.

In terms of sacramental performance, as exercised in conventional churches, the tension will prevail between conventional Christians who, for the greater part, wish to receive passively from the divinely endowed pastor, and the more adult spiritual seeker desiring deeper levels of mutual participation, creative involvement, along with a focus on real life issues, in a context where the priest or liturgist is viewed more as a facilitator rather than one who presides. Presiding carries connotations of power-over, whereas facilitating wisdom aims at openness and receptivity to the mutuality of shared power for the benefit and empowerment of all.

For Personal/Group Reflection

- What attracts you to the church or causes you to struggle with it?
- How has your understanding of church changed over the years?
- Rather than taking the Gospels literally, we need to interpret them in pursuit of deeper meaning. How do lay people prepare for this challenge?
- At the local level, how do you reimagine a church more open to, and receptive of, the needs of questioning adults?
- List six features you would consider important for an adult-inspiring church.

Chapter Six

Faith in the Future

Anticipation is what bears the universe along as it reaches out toward fuller being.

— John F. Haught

It is our imagination that allows us to give form to the Spirit's urgings.

— Judy Cannato

It is March 2025 as Rohan awakens to another day of trans-global communication. Rohan is an Indian brain surgeon who today will join three teams performing delicate surgery on three different continents: Asia, South America, and Europe. And for Rohan it all happens within the confines of his small home-based office in Mumbai, India.

Using advanced visualization technology, Rohan first links up with the surgical team in Beijing, China. A young woman has internal bleeding from her brain. Rohan activates his telepresence unit and within seconds is connected with the theater where surgeons have already opened the young woman's skull. Rohan directs the holographic representation attached to the on-site camera with which he can clearly detect the site of the bleeding. He then activates the robotic instruments and begins to gently manipulate the brain tissue. Speaking in his native Hindi, Rohan leads the team, who interpret what he is saying in their native Cantonese, thanks to instantaneous translation technology. Within two hours the bleeding has been arrested, and the team continue to reconstruct the young woman's brain. Rohan enjoys a relaxing lunch on the balcony of his small house, as he anticipates his afternoon consultation, this time with a team in Santiago, Chile.

This is a much more complicated case, a young man with a brain tumor. Three hours of deep conversation—this time Hindi translated into Spanish—determines the strategy for the best chance of a successful outcome. Surgery will follow the next day with Rohan eavesdropping on the procedure in an advisory capacity.

It is time for Rohan to have a quick evening meal before hooking up with his colleagues in Great Ormonde children's hospital in London, UK, working under intense time pressure on a young child with a suspected brain tumor. On this occasion, Rohan is a consultant observer, accompanying the team throughout the delicate procedure lasting six and a half hours. It is well after midnight, and Rohan, feeling very tired, but also very pleased, lies down to rest.

Such is life in the day of a typical surgeon living in 2025, and in many cases it will be much more amazing and surprising than depicted in this imaginary scenario. However, there is a downside, and this is where we reconnect with the adult and the additional discerning wisdom needed in this cyberspace environment.

I borrow Rohan's story from the intriguing analysis of future work patterns as depicted by the British business entrepreneur Lynda Gratton (2011, 78ff.). Gratton highlights the disturbing sense of social isolation that is likely to accompany this new work strategy in our cyberspace age. On a typical day, Rohan may never move outside the confines of his own home. Although connected globally with several colleagues in some groundbreaking medical endeavors, his social network may be extremely restricted, and his capacity for intimate relationships may be seriously limited. The hectic, exciting pace could all too easily become a camouflage for a lonely isolation, potentially destructive to Rohan's social, emotional, and spiritual development.

In the Hands of the Future

Spiritual traditions tend to encourage a focus on the here and now: live in the present moment. Allegedly, this is the stance that protects us from being stuck in the false securities of the past or nervously preoccupied about the prospects of the future. It is a focus associated with trust in providence, attentiveness to the present moment, and transparency to the divine in the encounter of the here and now. It is an outlook popularized in our time by such best sellers as Eckhart Tolle's *The Power of Now*. It has an obvious appeal, presenting an ideal much documented but rarely realized in practice.

Quantum physics helps us appreciate afresh the continuous nature of time, the flow from past through present and on to the future. Darwinian evolution, on the one hand, and conventional religion, on the other, both highlight the significance of the past, assuring us that all that is true and authentic is built on the past, and therefore the greatest assurance of authenticity comes by honoring the continuity with the past. Spirituality highlights the importance of the present moment. All of which leaves us with an ambiguous sense of *the future*, construed as vague and elusive, something we wait upon, an emerging reality we deal with as it begins to unfold.

For people grappling with adult meaning in our rapidly changing world, the future feels important. So important, in fact, it deserves a more conscious sense of engagement, not to be taken for granted or entrusted to a destiny lying in the laps of the gods. A more creative, conscious engagement with the future involves a number of processes that are both psychological and spiritual in nature.

1. We are creatures programmed to draw meaning from the future. It is our dreams, hopes, and aspirations that endow our future with purpose and hope.

2. A will to meaning underpins all human behavior. The creative energy that constitutes the foundational reality of our lives, while biologically driven from the past, evolves into greater complexity under the impact of the evolutionary lure of the future (further elaboration below).

3. Unknowingly for the greater part, we live out of the future. It is the dimension in the flow of life that motivates and inspires our every effort.

4. A more informed commitment to the future involves conscious choice to embrace change as a central dynamic of evolutionary growth and development.

5. Change involves breakthrough, but also breakdown. No transformative change is possible without embracing the great cycle of birth-death-rebirth that characterizes all life-forms, human and nonhuman.

6. The future is unpredictable and has to be that way in an evolving universe endowed with freedom and creativity. The unpredictability need not be some kind of curse, as postulated by popular religiosity, but a challenge requiring a quality of wisdom and skill largely undeveloped in our modern consciousness.

7. Humans strive to create a future of their own making and find it notoriously difficult to acknowledge an evolutionary imperative that provides foundational wisdom. When it comes to the unfolding of the future, we are not really in charge; a wisdom greater than ours is guiding the process—and it does not have to be a divine life-force as conventionally understood.

It is the last point in the above list that is evoking a new adult consciousness in our time. There is a growing weariness and disillusionment with all the human attempts—secular and religious—to control the world in which we live. And most illusive of all are our attempts to control the future. Our world and its resources are being held ransom by an addiction of control. Driven by fierce competition and petrified angst about our very survival, we invest an enormous amount of energy doing all the things that continue to deplete our energy and that lock us into ever more destructive ways of being, alienating us from the very womb that has begotten and sustains us.

Paradoxically, it is not a firmer grip on the past or on the present that will save us from perdition, but a greater openness to the future, trust in evolution's unfolding process, and a willingness to serve an evolving wisdom greater than anything we can conceive or imagine. In the language of many great mystics, our hope rests in divine abandonment, and not in insatiable grasping and clinging to "certainties" that become ever more opaque and unreliable.

Investing Hope in Technology

Ilia Delio provides an impressively informed analysis of how technology affects the modern human psyche, along with possible developments for the future of human evolution (2013, 155–76). For many of our contemporaries: "Technology has come to define who and what we are; it has become the mirror of our deepest desires" (Delio 2013, 156). We are heavily dependent on a vast range of technological resources, ranging from kitchen design to office equipment to medical procedures to mechanical accessories for almost every aspect of our daily lives. But what is alarming is the potential impact on the meaning of human identity.

The term *posthuman* was first highlighted by cultural theorist Ihab Hassan in his 1977 essay "Prometheus as Performer: Toward a Posthuman Culture?" (Hassan 1977). The concept was further explored in the mid-1980s by scholars such as Donna Haraway, Judith Halberstam, and N. Katherine Hayles. In her book *How We Became Posthuman*, Hayles argues that one becomes posthuman as soon as one enters a "cybernetic circuit that splices [one's] will, desire, and perception into a distributed cognitive system in which represented bodies are joined with enacted bodies through mutating and flexible machine interfaces" (Hayles 1999, 193). This interface of human and machine was later named *the cyborg* by Donna Haraway.

The London Paralympics of August 2012 extensively demonstrated the transformative influence of technology for human empowerment and creativity. In a less ostentatious manner such hybridity had already been influencing human life and well-being. Already in 1958, medical scientists in Sweden devised the first implantable pacemaker. Despite the fact that the patient, Arne Larsson, subsequently went on to receive twenty-six different pacemakers, he lived till 2001, reaching the ripe age of eighty-six years. Had Arne Larsson not received the pacemaker presumably he would have died many years previously, raising a range of philosophical and ethical questions not merely about the meaning of life and death, but about the very identity of being a human-cum-machine person—whose life destiny may be altered significantly thanks to technological advances of our time.

Ray Kurzweil (2005) is an oft-cited futurist, who predicts that by the middle of the twenty-first century humans will be capable of obtaining *nanobots* (tiny technological programs that may not even be visible to the human eye) that can be bodily inserted (possibly by oneself), with the capability to modify aspects of human behavior and well-being that currently are totally beyond human modification. With good reason, reflective humans shudder at the very thought of such a preposterous outcome. It becomes all the more scary when we consider that governments may be incapable of controlling such runaway technological adventures.

Millions, currently absorbed in the cyber-informational culture of our time, invest enormous hope in the information revolution. Delio states that "many transhumanists look to a post-biological future where super informational beings will flourish" (2013, 161). For such people, the future of evolution is in the power of technology—not merely as the resource to rectify all the major problems of our age, but to deliver a vastly improved quality of life for future humans.

This is a vision riddle with paradoxical prospects, one that bewilders several reflective adults today and will prove a mammoth challenge for the discerning minds and hearts of the future. First, the allurement of such technology has a dangerously narrow anthropocentric slant to it; frequently little consideration is allowed for all the other creatures who share the web of life with us or for the well-being of the planet. Second, the superpowers who will both patronize and police such developments are a largely unknown entity, currently likely to be megacorporations driven by greed and self-aggrandizement. Third, however, there is a paradoxical factor that can sustain a meaningful sense of hope while presenting an enormous challenge for contemplative gaze and wise discernment.

This third insight I highlight with a quote from the modern posthumanist scholar Elaine Graham:

> Human beings have always coevolved with their environments, tools and technologies. By that I mean that to be human is already to be in a web of relationships, where our humanity can only be articulated—realized—in and through our environment, our tools, our artefacts, and the networks of human and non-human life around us. It also means that we do not need to be afraid of our complicity with technologies or fear our hybridity or assume that proper knowledge of and access to God can only come through a withdrawal from these activities of world-building. (Graham 2004, 25)

I find it difficult to share such forthright optimism—until I remind myself that in all probability my human ancestors were also fearful of, and cynical about, the breakthroughs of earlier evolutionary epochs. It is only with hindsight that any generation is likely to see the fuller advantages of significant change.

Technology is an integral dimension of coevolution at this time and will remain so for the foreseeable future. It is an aspect of the lure of the future that we resist to our own detriment, as intimated by the physicist Michio Kaku (2011) in a highly informed analysis. Instead, we need to embrace it, mobilizing our individual and collective resources to provide the necessary wisdom and discernment, while committing ourselves to the ongoing development of our critical and discerning faculties—combined with new social and political skills—to evolve strategies and structures that will channel this breakthrough to the benefit of person and planet alike. This indeed is a formidable and daunting undertaking, and we don't have the right to opt out. Time alone will tell if we can rise to the challenge. When it comes to adult-based faith, this is certainly a new threshold requiring a quality of resilience and wisdom largely unknown in the modern world.

What Do We Mean by the Future?

For more reflective adults, the future is a great deal more complex and unpredictable than is generally assumed in our public and political policies. Evolution plays a crucial role, and it involves a great deal more than the well-worn cliché of "the survival of the fittest." We target potential winners and invest our resources in them, on the unquestioned assumption that everybody will eventually enjoy the beneficial outcomes. What is becoming increasingly clear—and disturbing to more intuitive adults—is that power games are at the heart of this process, and the powerful are the ones who benefit most, ultimately creating a worldwide culture benefiting neither the majority of humans nor the living earth itself.

As we strive to discern evolution's future thrust, two important correctives are coming to the fore: First is the need to appropriate a more generic understanding of *evolution*, devoid of so much of the ideological propaganda that accompanies the concept in current usage. Second, how evolution unfolds—particularly with reference to the future—needs to be freshly revisioned. As already indicated, I find the overviews provided by Ilia Delio (2013) and Carter Phipps (2012) to be particularly inspiring for the envisaged readership of this book.

I think we can cut through a great deal of ideological rhetoric by adopting *a basic definition of evolution* as a process of *growth-change-development*. Viewing the natural world around us, we see things growing, a vast range of life-forms becoming and developing through greater complexity. The growth involves a continuous process of change and alteration, and this implies death and rebirth. It is often an untidy, messy process and certainly does not follow a neat logical progression. Any process of development involving increasing levels of complexity, elegance, and beauty will be accompanied by a considerable amount of destruction and waste. At every level of life, creation and destruction are interwoven in evolution's trajectory.

There is a widespread assumption—in both the academic world and in conventional wisdom—that the entire process is driven from the past and essentially builds on the achievements of earlier stages. The future is assumed to flow out of the past. Consequently, a great deal of attention is focused on the past and what works well, particularly that which triumphs and endures. We assume that the resilient achievements of the past will become the foundational basis for everything that transpires thereafter.

Almost singlehandedly, within the Western academic world, John Haught, former professor of theology at Georgetown University, has challenged the prevailing understanding of evolution positing instead *a lure of the future* which, he claims, is foundational to the entire process of evolution, personal and planetary (Haught 2010). Not merely is life driven from successful achievements of the past, but it is pulled toward the future by forces at work within the cosmic, evolutionary process that humans cannot control. In Haught's view *the lure of the future* is at least every bit as significant as the imprint of the past, a conviction that does not endear him to scientific colleagues but one with a deepening sense of authenticity for adult faith seekers of our time.

Anyone familiar with John Haught's thinking will readily recognize his competence not merely in theology but also in a range of evolutionary sciences, including neo-Darwinianism. Consistently, he affirms the insights of Charles Darwin and many of the subsequent scientific developments of Darwin's key ideas; Haught goes on to build on these foundations, emphasizing what he perceives to be a seriously missing dimension, namely *the future lure.* Haught is an interdisciplinary scholar, an approach endorsed by several academic institutions, but often scathingly undermined when applied to real life situations. It is this multidisciplinary approach that appeals—consciously and subconsciously—to adult faith seekers today.

Haught builds his new ideas around the Christian notion that the God we believe in is a God of promises who always remains faithful to his word. Obviously, this is a theological conviction, one that Haught develops almost exclusively in a Christian context. Expanding these ideas, *the lure of the future* is the invitation of God's Holy Spirit to be open and hospitable to the new future that God always makes possible for us humans—and for the creation we inhabit. In the words of Ilia Delio, "The foundation of things is not so much a ground of being sustaining its existence from beneath as it is a power of attraction toward *what lies ahead*" (2013, 18); and "God is not so much behind creation as its cause, but in front of creation as its future" (128). The ensuing challenge—for Christians and others alike—is to engage with the divine initiative in the ongoing work of coevolution. Theologians such as Philip Heffner (1993) name it as the task of *co-creation*.

A New Theological Threshold

Several new departure points are woven into this notion of future impact and inspiration. I have met many adults who intuitively were aware of these ideas but were either unsure of them or unable to bring them into speech. Sometimes, it was a struggle to find the right language, but more frequently it was a long lurking fear of being deluded and misguided, a fear of being misunderstood, of being perceived as a traitor to one's faith or to one's church. In our modern culture, such fear may seem irrational, and even primitive. We need to remember that its deep-seated hold on our consciousness belongs to a codependent dynamic that has dominated our Western consciousness for several centuries. It will not be easily or quickly dislodged.

Positively, we embrace the challenge of trusting those inner questings, and the alternative insights that accompany them. Next, as outlined in chapter 1, we seek forums of kindred spirits where we can share our stories and give voice (maybe for the first time) to intuitions that have been awakening within us for many years. These inner hunches may include all or some of the following awakenings:

1. *Revelation.* Contrary to the formal theological assertion that revelation belongs primarily to the Judeo-Christian tradition, and effectively ended with the death of the last apostle, adult faith seekers consider that view far too anthropocentric (human-focused), and it feels dangerously close to humans trying to control God. Instead they eagerly embrace the view propounded by the Thomas Berry (2006) that revelation belongs to the whole process of cosmic-planetary creation, and—further inspired by modern science—it is taking place in a world without beginning or end (an infinite universe).

2. *Continuity.* In all the religions, those truths that are firmly rooted in the past are considered to be authentic and foundational. Moreover, all development of "doctrine" should follow a linear line of emergence, always building on the past, and never abandoning the truth of earlier times. For contemporary adults this is too linear, rational, and anthropocentric. Adults suspect that patriarchal control dominates the process. Openness to a new and different future—over which humans may have little or no control—is considered significantly important for our time.

3. *The Human Condition.* In the 1990s, people participating in human growth programs sometimes adopted the slogan: "God is not finished

with me yet." Adults, appropriating a more spiritual view of life, become increasingly uneasy and impatient with the prevailing developmental philosophy that deems biology and genetics as primary determining factors of all that defines and constitutes our humanity. Such people intuit that there is a deep mystery to our humanity and our unfolding, individually and collectively; we are not merely conditioned by our past, but respond even more dynamically to several creative urges from the future.

4. *Worldviews.* For several centuries now, most humans have been indoctrinated in an anthropocentric ideology. Humans comes first, endowed with a wisdom transcending all other creatures and the planet itself. Humans can intelligently use the power of reason, which no other organism can do. That entitles us to treat and appropriate all other life-forms for our use and benefit. A growing cohort of contemporary adults are highly suspicious of this ideology. It feels too narrow and utilitarian to be real. In the light of the emerging wisdom of our time—even within the academic domain itself—it is a worldview that is no longer sustainable or meaningful.

5. *Whom Do We Trust?* This is becoming an engaging and disturbing question for many contemporary adults. Among both youth and older people we experience a growing distrust of those in charge, whether in politics, economics, religion, or social policy. In our world of mass

information, the human mind is sharper and more critical. So much more information is now widely available! More adults trust intuition and the creative imagination. More people want to be involved in co-creating a different—and hopefully, a better—future, not on the basis of reliable knowledge from the past, but on the basis of the amorphous wisdom that characterizes our time, despite all the contradictions and chaotic elements that belong to the awakening consciousness.

Lured Toward What?

Humans are no longer viewed as passive observers of a divine patriarch governing in a domineering and controlling way from a distant heaven. Taking incarnation far more seriously, humans are invited and challenged to become co-creators with our creative God who works creatively and collaboratively in the power of living Spirit, embodied in all life-forms, including the living earth and the universe to which we all belong. Instead of waiting on God to work redemptive miracles to make the world a better place, inspired by the living example of Jesus (for Christians), we need to assume the responsibility for the work of global and personal transformation. The challenge is boldly affirmed in these words from the Scripture scholar John Dominic Crossan:

> We owe it to God to run God's world responsibly. We owe the divine Householder the conservation of the world house; we owe the divine Homemaker the con-

secration of the earth home. We owe God adequate care of all God's creation. We owe God collaboration in honoring God's name, in establishing God's kingdom, and in doing God's will "as in heaven so also on earth." We owe it to God to cease focusing on heaven, especially in order to avoid focusing on earth. (Crossan 2010, 155)

This new challenge appeals deeply to contemporary people of adult faith, although practically it poses a complex and daunting challenge.

What then is the future we are invited to co-create afresh? And what is the lure that can nourish and sustain us in that endeavor? The following seem to be some of the key elements:

- Evolutionary unfolding follows an intelligence inherent in the process of evolution itself. We humans need to become much more aware of and attuned to that emergent process.
- Divine wisdom is innate in that process, not as an anthropocentric form of control from the past, but rather as a lure inviting all living creatures into a process of co-creation for a better future.
- To engage meaningfully in this creative process, humans need to learn a spirituality of befriending and forgo our compulsion for control and domination.
- We need to develop an ecology of being a servant species to a complex creation that will flourish abetted by our collaboration rather

than one continuously subjected to our destructive anthropocentric domination. (For more, see the inspiring synthesis of Christie 2013.)

- As the creative Spirit lures us forth, we need to be open to ever new learnings on all aspects of the web of life.
- Our politics, economics, technology, and the construction of social reality will need to be revisioned in ways that will honor multidisciplinary wisdom, with not merely the good of people as the primary goal, but the advancement of the entire web of life.
- Formal religion will need to let go of its dogmatic certainties and trust the Spirit who blows where it will, always luring us toward a more open-ended future.
- Churches will need to become communities skilled in contemplative wisdom and deep dialogue, so that we can discern more clearly the ways in which the living Spirit is luring forth not merely humans, but the cosmic creation in all its future possibilities.

For Personal/Group Reflection

- How do you understand the phrase "having faith in the future"?
- As an adult exploring a deeper sense of faith, how does your faith nourish a meaningful sense of the future?
- What personal meaning do you glean from John Haught's idea of the lure of the future?

- What future structures might be necessary to promote and develop adult faith development?
- Is it possible to engage formal churches (religions) in the type of adult faith development outlined in this book?

Adult Adjustments for the Church of the South

In 1960, 66 percent of the Catholic population of the world lived in the West, predominantly in the northern hemisphere of Europe and North America. That means that 34 percent were residing in the South, mainly in Central and South America. In 2012, the demographics have changed dramatically. Out of a total Catholic population of 1.2 billion, an estimated 80 percent live in the South (Central and South America, Africa, Asia), resulting in a mere 20 percent residing in the church of the West.

I examine this demographic shift as a Catholic phenomenon, noting that it parallels a similar trend in other Christian denominations. Since many of the readers of this book are likely to be Catholics, I focus primarily on the challenges arising for Catholic adults today. As I shall indicate presently, the challenges will differ significantly in terms of the West and the South.

Discerning the Shift

I hope the reader feels surprised, if not shocked, by that massive shift in a mere fifty years. Nobody set out to bring this about, and many analysts are quick to offer explanations related to shifts in population and a range of socioeconomic factors. I suspect they are missing a crucial insight. As a believing Christian, I veer toward a religious explanation, beginning with a simple but profound question: *Is the Holy Spirit within and behind this movement?* I answer *affirmatively!* Once one makes such a discernment, one quickly realizes the enormous implications of what is transpiring for Catholics worldwide in our time.

This rapid shift to the South suggests that the Holy Spirit is birthing a new church for a radical new Catholic future. This might well mark the end of the church of Constantine (prevalent since the fourth century) and the refounding of a church more authentically aligned with the Companionship of Empowerment (the Kingdom of God). The West is no longer the primary wellspring, and Rome is no longer the heart-center of the Catholic Church today. In fact, there is probably more than one heart-center. An initial glance at the Catholic spread in the South indicates that the Philippines (for Asia), Nigeria (for Africa) and Brazil (for Central and South America) are likely to emerge as the new heart-centers.

This is a new hour of grace for the Catholic Church, the likes of which has not been known since the Christian faith first evolved more than two thousand years ago. In fact, it is the first serious dent in the church that became so addicted to the imperialism of Constantine. There is no blueprint to follow, other than a concerted attempt of seeking hearts and discerning minds. It is the newness of this transition that is particularly challenging for a church with such a weighted preference for the past, for tradition, for the old.

Breakdown and Breakthrough

The emergence of the church in the South raises a range of disturbing and profound questions for contemporary adult faith seekers. And the challenge to engage in appropriate discernment is formidable, one that even adult seekers have not named or embraced. We are quick to look askance at the church in the South with its predominantly conservative ethos, its heavy reliance on clerical power, and its extensive appropriation of Western European modes of behavior, pastoral practice, formation training, and prevailing moral guidelines. Faced with these all too obvious contradictions, the adult rightly asks: How can we claim that the Holy Spirit is operative in such an oppressive ecclesiastical climate? Surely such a perception must be false, or at the very least inadequate?

Paradoxically, the signs of life and vitality that appeal to adults are much more obvious in the church of the West, despite the regressive nature of church leadership in the closing decades of the twentieth century, the decline in numbers, the aging profile, and the demoralization arising from clerical sex abuse. Adult people still find spaces and opportunities to exercise ministry in creative and active ways—with options that simply are not available in many parts of the church of the South.

To discern what the Spirit is up to, I suggest we embrace the spirituality of the Paschal Journey, with its baffling paradox of destruction-cum-creation, the recurring cycle of birth-death-new life. When we look at the Christian dynamic of death and resurrection, we note that the initial seeds of resurrection hope sprout from within the Calvary experience itself. Jesus always combines Calvary with Resurrection in his attempts to prepare his followers for this transitional experience. Today, the church of the West is undergoing crucifixion, most obvious in the demise of clerical priesthood, the aging profile, and the sex-abuse scandals. Not surprising, therefore, it is in this same space of death—understood in paschal terms—that adults often experience possibilities for new life and meaning.

Logically, we expect the new endeavors to come from the South, but the Spirit works with a dynamic much bigger and deeper than human logic. The future of Catholicism most definitely belongs to the South, and not to the West, where diminishment and death will continue unabated. The new flourishing of empowering faith that the Spirit seeks to awaken thus far is manifesting more publicly and lucidly in the North—amid the death and dying—rather than in the South. However, if those new awakenings are to blossom into their full potential, it will be the creativity of the South rather than the West that will guarantee that outcome. And I believe that the Spirit will eventually engineer that breakthrough—in the South rather than the West.

Adult Options

Adult people of faith in the South need to wake up to the challenge staring them in the face. The Spirit is calling forth a

quality and quantity of response that will be dauntingly difficult for Southerners to adopt, and yet it is crucial for Catholics
all over the world that our colleagues in the South take those
brave adult options. These formidable challenges include:

- Stop mimicking Europe and the West and devote your creative energy to co-creating structures, liturgies, and pastoral practices congenial
  to the indigenous wisdom of the South.
- To continue talking about Rome—and judging
  orthodoxy by Roman criteria—is a classic example of seeking the living among the dead (see
  Luke 24:5). The Gospel now needs to be rooted
  in the Wisdom of the South.
- Return primary allegiance to the Companionship
  of Empowerment (the Kingdom of God), and facilitate a rebirth of the church as servant and her-
  ald of the new Companionship.
- The church as the people of God—with laity to
  the fore in every sphere—must be reclaimed as
  the primary meaning of the church of the South.
  In all probability the Holy Spirit wants this new
  face of the church to be radically lay—in all its
  major dimensions.
- All attachments to imperial clericalism (right back
  to the time of Constantine) need to be severed.
  A people's church, and not a priest-controlled
  church, needs to be brought into being.
- Sacraments need to be returned to the people
  (rather than reserved to the priest) and realigned
  with indigenous rites of passage.

- Gospel wisdom, sustaining a catechesis that will honor the new work of the Spirit, needs to be appropriated first and foremost by lay people, and not merely by priests.
- It is absolutely imperative that Southern Catholics (and Christians in general) embark on a program of lay formation, including a comprehensive grounding in Scripture, theology, and spirituality.

The pioneering adults of the new church in the South will need to remain firmly grounded in the spirituality of the paschal journey. They must not seek the living among the dead—that is to say, they must cease looking to the dying empire of the West for spiritual and theological inspiration. More important, they need to devote contemplative attention to the words of the angel (the archetypal wisdom) in Matthew 28:6–7.: *You will not encounter the Risen Christ here (in Rome, Europe, or the West); he goes before you into Galilee; it is there you will meet him.* Symbolically (and factually), Galilee is where Jesus first proclaimed the Kingdom of God, the foundational source of all Christian faith, the archetypal starting point for new life and empowering natality.

For faithful adults in the South the Risen One who goes ahead is the pioneering endeavor of the Holy Spirit, birthing a new church for the twenty-first century in the Southern hemisphere. Southerners en masse must now become the midwives to the church of the future. There is nothing to be gained by glancing back at Europe or the West—there is no new life there. The newness is in the South, and adult people of faith in the South must risk everything to grasp this unique moment of the church's refounding.

And where does all this leave the adults in the North or the West? In a painfully difficult place, requiring discerning skills and wisdom, thus far in short supply. Adults in the West must learn to befriend the death and dying in a dignified and active manner. Adults in the West must excel in the skills of cultural hospice care. How we deal with the death has implications too for our colleagues in the South. Within the paschal mystery, life and death are intimately interconnected.

Faithful adults in the West can draw much inspiration from the role of the women in the Calvary and Resurrection context. Whereas all the male apostles fled—they could not embrace the pain, the grief, and the mourning—the women stood steadfast and remained to the bitter end. And precisely because they stayed faithful to the bitter end—using the feminine intuitive wisdom to keep them focused—they were the first to enter the frightening but liberating space of resurrection promise.

To honor the grieving, the mourning, the dying—and to be active in burying the dead—adult people of faith in the West will need to develop discerning wisdom in the following areas:

- Adults will need education and formation on the psychological and spiritual dynamics of death and dying (as developed by scholars such as Elisabeth Kübler-Ross).
- Adults will need to be particularly vigilant on the use of creative energy. They must not waste energy on "analysing the parts to death" (Margaret J. Wheatley), in counterproductive words and actions around clericalized church life.

- New initiatives—in all areas of church life—need to be embraced boldly and subversively—inspired by the daring vision of the Gospel parables.
- Theological insights from lay theologians need to be prioritized over clericalized wisdom.
- Small group initiatives and ecclesial networking are likely to be the strategies that will sustain hope and meaning in the midst of the dying—the kind of initiatives pioneered by Saint Paul in early church development.
- Rituals of healing need to be adopted extensively to heal the wounds of ecclesiastical imperialism, particularly for women, and for all who feel victimized by the abuse of power.
- Adults in the West will need to be particularly attentive to the insights and wisdom of chaos theory. It will prove to be a sustaining resource in dealing with the death and dying.
- Adults must not be discouraged by the fierce resistance and intransigence of the institutional church, which is likely to resort to extreme measures in order to keep the grief from becoming visible, and to retain their own imperial status as things progressively fall apart.

The Middle Spirit

Undoubtedly, some readers will find these ideas bombastic, far-fetched, and alien to all sense of credulity. They also fly in the face of our prevailing pneumatology, which tends to depict the Holy Spirit as a principle of law and order, justifying the prevailing powers to exert their power and authority. The American theologian Shelly Rambo (2010) alerts us to another understanding of the Holy Spirit, also using the Paschal Journey as a primary context. We rush through the trauma of Good Friday, the low ebb of Holy Saturday, and the dark troublesome dawn of Easter morning (all the Gospels tell us that the women were filled with fear)—pressing ahead desperately to the feast of Pentecost when the Holy Spirit reassures us that all will be well.

In that process we miss what Shelly Rambo calls the *Middle Spirit*, the Spirit that befriends the pain, the anguish, the agony, the death, and dying. The Spirit also works through these negative experiences, inviting us to journey alongside brokenness, fragility, letting go, decline, and death—not just in human life but in our major institutions as well.

In our time the Holy Spirit is doing a new thing in both the West and the South. It is important to keep in mind the metaphors I have earlier adopted: that of the *hospice carer* for adults in the West and that of the *midwife* for adults in the South. In both areas the risks are great, the process is messy and untidy, and the stakes are high for a good quality of life. Struggle and pain are inherent in both pilgrim paths, and the engagement at times will push adults to the limits of their sanity. This is fertile territory for the Middle Spirit, where birth and death coexist, and the breakthrough for a new church cannot happen without the demise of the old imperial reality.

The Spirit Blows Where It Will . . .

I want to conclude this final section by invoking the power of creative imagination, one of the primary resources that adults—both in the West and South—will need if we are to befriend the Holy Spirit in a creative and authentic way. Let's give expression to what the awakening dream of the new church of the South might look like. Might a patriarchal papacy be replaced by a collaborative structure of *team leadership*, in which a team—of say twenty-one persons—would be made up of five Caucasians and sixteen nonwhites from the South, fourteen women and seven men, with an average age of about forty, honoring the youthfulness of the South. Sacramental practice would be returned to people's innate capacity for ritual making with clerical priesthood giving way to ritual leadership called forth from the body of believers. Leadership would prioritize animation over domination, inspiration over doctrinal control, and a global spirituality that would emphasize commonalities rather than differences.

And perhaps the biggest challenge of all would be the *calling forth of the adult*, among people who for far too long have been infantilized into passive submissive immaturity. Evangelization would recapture the Gospel vision of the Kingdom of God (the Companionship of Empowerment), and in the daring awakening of parabolic lore, people of adult faith would once more be challenged into codiscipleship with an adult Jesus serving an adult God.

Does it all sound too far-fetched? Can anything be too far-fetched for the Spirit who blows where she will?

Bibliography

Abram, David. 2010. *Becoming Animal: An Earthly Cosmology*, New York: Vintage Books.

Aquinas, St. Thomas. 1956. *Summa Contra Gentiles* ll,2.3, edited by Joseph Kenny. New York: Hanover House.

Armstrong, Karen. 1993. *A History of God: The 4,000-Year Quest of Judaism, Christianity, and Islam*. New York: A. A. Knopf.

Arnett, Jeffrey Jensen. 2002. *Adolescence and Emerging Adulthood*. Upper Saddle River, NJ: Prentice Hall.

Bateson, Mary Catherine. 2010. *Composing a Further Life: The Age of Active Wisdom*. New York: Alfred A. Knopf.

Berry, Thomas. 2006. *Evening Thoughts: Reflecting on Earth as Sacred Community*. San Francisco: Sierra Club Books.

Bevans, Stephen B., and Roger P. Schroeder. 2011. *Prophetic Dialogue: Reflections of Christian Mission Today*. Maryknoll, NY: Orbis Books.

Brock, Rita Nakashima, and Rebecca Ann Parker. 2008. *Saving Paradise: How Christianity Traded Love of This World for Crucifixion and Empire*. Boston: Beacon Press.

Bultmann, Rudolf. 1984. *The New Testament and Mythology and Other Basic Writings*. Philadelphia: Fortress Press.

Casey, Maurice. 2010. *Jesus of Nazareth: An Independent Historian's Account of His Life and Teaching*. New York: T&T Clark.

Childs, Hal. 2000. *The Myth of the Historical Jesus and the Evolution of Consciousness*. Atlanta: Society of Biblical Literature.

Christie, Douglas E. 2013. *The Blue Sapphire of the Mind: Notes for a Contemplative Ecology.* New York: Oxford University Press.

Crosby, Michael H. 1991. *The Dysfunctional Church: Addiction and Codependency in the Family of Catholicism.* Notre Dame, IN: Ave Maria Press. Republished in 2011 by Wipf & Stock, Eugene, Oregon.

Crossan, John Dominic. 2010. *The Greatest Prayer: Rediscovering the Revolutionary Message of the Lord's Prayer.* New York: Harper-One.

Delio, Ilia. 2013. *The Unbearable Wholeness of Being: God, Evolution, and the Power of Love.* Maryknoll, NY: Orbis Books.

Eisenstein, Charles. 2011. *Sacred Economics: Money, Gift, and Society in the Age of Transition.* Berkeley, CA: Evolver Editions.

Erikson, Erik H. 1959. *Identity and the Life Cycle: Selected Papers.* With a historical introduction by David Rapaport. New York: International Universities Press.

Fowler, James. 1981. *Stages of Faith: The Psychology of Human Development and the Quest for Meaning.* San Francisco: Harper and Row.

Fox, Patricia A. 2001. *God as Communion: John Zizioulas, Elizabeth Johnson, and the Retrieval of the Symbol of the Triune God.* Collegeville, MN: Liturgical Press.

Graham, Elaine. 2004. "Post/Human Conditions." *Theology and Sexuality* 10 (2): 10–32.

Gratton, Lynda. 2011. *The Shift: The Future of Work Is Already Here.* London: HarperCollins.

Harpur, Tom. 2004. *The Pagan Christ: Recovering the Lost Light.* Toronto: Thomas Allen.

Harris, Sam. 2005. *The End of Faith: Religion, Terror, and the Future of Reason.* New York: Norton.

Hassan, Ihab. 1977. "Prometheus as Performer: Toward a Posthumanist Culture?" *Georgia Review* 31 (4): 830–50.

Hathaway, Mark, and Leonardo Boff. 2009. *The Tao of Liberation: Exploring the Ecology of Transformation.* Maryknoll, NY: Orbis Books.

Haught, John F. 2010. *Making Sense of Evolution: Darwin, God, and the Drama of Life.* Louisville, KY: Westminster John Knox Press.

Hawken, Paul. 2007. *Blessed Unrest: How the Largest Movement in the World Came into Being, and Why No One Saw It Coming.* New York: Viking.

Hayles, Katherine N. 1999. *How We Became Posthuman: Virtual Bodies in Cybernetics, Literature, and Informatics.* Chicago: University of Chicago Press.

Heffner, Philip. 1993. *The Human Factor: Evolution, Culture and Religion.* Minneapolis: Fortress Press.

Hoffman, Virginia Curran. 1991. *The Codependent Church.* New York: Crossroad.

Johnson, Elizabeth A. 2007. *Quest for the Living God: Mapping Frontiers in the Theology of God.* New York: Continuum.

Kaku, Michio. 2011. *Physics of the Future: How Science Will Shape Human Destiny and Our Daily Lives by the Year 2100.* New York: Doubleday.

Keller, Catherine. 2003. *Face of the Deep: A Theology of Becoming.* London: Routledge.

————. 2008. *On the Mystery: Discerning Divinity in Process.* Minneapolis: Fortress Press.

Kurzweil, Ray. 2005. *The Singularity Is Near: When Humans Transcend Biology.* New York: Viking.

LaCugna, Catherine Mowry. 1991. *God for Us: The Trinity and Christian Life.* San Francisco: HarperSanFrancisco.

Le Grice, Keiron. 2010. *The Archetypal Cosmos: Rediscovering the Gods in Myth, Science and Astrology.* Edinburgh: Floris Books.

Moltmann, Jürgen. 1992. *The Spirit of Life: A Universal Affirmation.* Translated by Margaret Kohl. Minneapolis: Fortress Press.

Moss, Candida. 2013. *The Myth of Persecution,* New York: HarperCollins.

Nelson-Pallmeyer, Jack. 2003. *Is Religion Killing Us? Violence in the Bible and the Quran.* Harrisburg, PA: Trinity Press International.

O'Murchu, Diarmuid. 2008. *Ancestral Grace: Meeting God in Our Human Story.* Maryknoll, NY: Orbis Books.

————. 2010. *Adult Faith: Growing in Wisdom and Understanding.* Maryknoll, NY: Orbis Books.

————. 2011. *Christianity's Dangerous Memory: A Rediscovery of the Revolutionary Jesus.* New York: Crossroad.

————. 2012. *In the Beginning Was the Spirit: Science, Religion, and Indigenous Spirituality.* Maryknoll, NY: Orbis Books.

Page, Nick. 2012. *Kingdom of Fools: The Unlikely Rise of the Early Church.* London: Hodder & Stoughton.

Pérez Esclarín, Antonio. 1978. *Atheism and Liberation.* Translated by John Drury. Maryknoll, NY: Orbis Books.

Phipps, Carter. 2012. *Evolutionaries*. New York: Harper Perennial.

Plotkin, Bill. 2008. *Nature and the Human Soul: Cultivating Wholeness and Community in a Fragmented World*. Novato, CA: New World Library.

Polkinghorne, John, ed. 2010. *The Trinity and an Entangled World: Relationality in Physical Science and Theology*. Grand Rapids, MI: Eerdmans.

Rambo, Shelly. 2010. *Spirit and Trauma: A Theology of Remaining*. Louisville, KY: Westminster John Knox Press.

Rohr, Richard. 2011. *Falling Upward: A Spirituality for the Two Halves of Life*. San Francisco: Jossey-Bass.

Roszak, Theodore. 2001. *The Longevity Revolution: As Boomers Become Elders*. Berkeley, CA: Berkeley Hills Books.

———. 2009. *The Making of an Elder Culture: Reflections on the Future of America's Most Audacious Generation*. Gabriola Island, BC: New Society Publishers.

Sanders, E. P. 1985. *Jesus and Judaism*. Minneapolis: Fortress Press.

Sheehan, Thomas. 1986. *The First Coming: How the Kingdom of God Became Christianity*. New York: Random House.

Smith, Christian, and Patricia Snell. 2009. *Souls in Transition: The Religious and Spiritual Lives of Emerging Adults*. New York: Oxford University Press.

Tarnas, Richard. 2006. *Cosmos and Psyche: Intimations of a New World View*. New York: Viking.

Taylor, John V. 1972. *The Go-Between God: The Holy Spirit and the Christian Mission*. London: SCM Press.

Vermès, Géza. 1973. *Jesus the Jew: A Historian's Reading of the Gospels*. London: Collins.

Wallace, Mark I. 2005. *Finding God in the Singing River: Christianity, Spirit, Nature*. Minneapolis: Fortress Press.

Wink, Walter. 2002. *The Human Being: Jesus and the Enigma of the Son of Man*. Minneapolis: Fortress Press.

Winter, Miriam Therese. 2009. *Paradoxology: Spirituality in a Quantum Universe*. Maryknoll, NY: Orbis Books.

Zizioulas, Jean. 2006. *Communion and Otherness: Further Studies in Personhood and the Church*. London: T&T Clark.